SUSTAINABLE YOUTH MINISTRY

Why most youth ministry doesn't last
and what your church can do about it

MARK DeVRIES

IVP Books

An imprint of InterVarsity Press
Downers Grove, Illinois

InterVarsity Press
P.O. Box 1400, Downers Grove, IL 60515-1426
ivpress.com
email@ivpress.com

©2008 by Mark DeVries

InterVarsity Press® is the book-publishing division of InterVarsity Christian Fellowship/USA®, a movement of students and faculty active on campus at hundreds of universities, colleges and schools of nursing in the United States of America, and a member movement of the International Fellowship of Evangelical Students. For information about local and regional activities, visit intervarsity.org.

All Scripture quotations, unless otherwise indicated, are taken from the Holy Bible, New International Version®. NIV®. Copyright ©1973, 1978, 1984 by International Bible Society. Used by permission of Zondervan Publishing House. All rights reserved.

Figure 6 on page 103 is from payscale.com. Used by permission.

Design: Cindy Kiple
Images: Nael Nabil/iStockphoto

ISBN 978-0-8308-3361-0

Printed in the United States of America ∞

 As a member of the Green Press Initiative, InterVarsity Press is committed to protecting the environment and to the responsible use of natural resources. To learn more, visit greenpressinitiative.org.

Library of Congress Cataloging-in-Publication Data

DeVries, Mark.
  Sustainable youth ministry: why most youth ministry doesn't last
  and what your church can do about it / Mark Devries.
    p. cm.
  Includes bibliographical references.
  ISBN 978-0-8308-3361-0 (pbk.: alk. paper)
  1. Church work with youth. I. Title.
  BV4447.D457 2008
  259'.23—dc22
                          2008031403

P   23   22   21   20   19   18   17   16   15

Y   27   26   25   24   23   22   21   20   19   18   17

To Jim and Donna Robers,

who taught an attention-deficit youth worker

the powerful leverage of structure,

who modeled a compelling reverence

for God and love for family,

and whose humor, friendship and wisdom

kept me in ministry long after others

recommended I give up

CONTENTS

A ROLL OF THE DICE

Exposing Today's Most Popular Youth Ministry Model

To live through an impossible situation, you don't need the reflexes of a Grand Prix driver, the muscles of Hercules, the mind of Einstein. You simply need to know what to do.

ANTHONY GREENBANK, *THE BOOK OF SURVIVAL*

My friend who owns the coffee shops told us, in a tone of kindness and truth, that nobody he knows who is successful gambles; rather they work hard, they accept the facts of reality, they enjoy life as it is. "But the facts really stink," I told him. "Reality is like a fine wine," he said to me. "It will not appeal to children."

DONALD MILLER, *SEARCHING FOR GOD KNOWS WHAT*

Over lunch at a restaurant in his college town, the twenty-year-old graduate of our youth ministry let me in on his dirty little secret.

He was scared, terrified actually. He had gotten in trouble, gotten involved with the wrong kind of people; he knew better. But the siren song had been too strong to resist. Undeniably hooked on gambling, he kept thinking he'd be able to win back everything he'd lost, if only he could just get into a big game. Well, he got in some big games, but win he didn't.

And so, with shaking hands, he looked across the table at me, confessing that he would soon be leaving school and trying to "keep a low profile," particularly from the organized crime ring that had loaned him somewhere in the neighborhood of twenty thousand dollars to stay in the game.

It reminded me, well, of youth ministry.

A LOOK AT TODAY'S MOST POPULAR
YOUTH MINISTRY MODEL

Each year, our Youth Ministry Architects team is privileged to work intimately with dozens of churches, partnering with them in building sustainable youth ministries. The more churches we have worked with, the more we have discovered patterns. By far the most startling is this: most American churches have, often without recognizing it, embraced a clear model for youth ministry, a model more popular than purpose-driven, family-based or contemplative. Most churches have chosen to do youth ministry with a model best described as gambling.

It looks like this: The leaders of the church cross their fingers and believe, with all their hearts, that *this time* the cards will fall in their favor. This time, they'll find the superstar youth director who will change everything . . . fast. This time, they'll find just the right curriculum, just the right convention that will, finally, make youth ministry *work* as it has never really worked before, at least not in a sustainable way. This time when they roll the dice, if they wish hard enough, a thriving youth ministry will turn up.

But few people get rich gambling. For every one that does, there are thousands mired in chronic poverty. But wealth—and sustainable youth ministry—come not from gambling but predictably from a strategic, sacrificial and annoyingly inconvenient investment of time and resources.

So if you're looking for a book that can give you easy steps for building a thriving youth ministry in the next three months, I'm afraid you've picked the wrong one. Oh, there are steps (and rest assured I'll be giving them to you), but they're anything but quick, and on occasion, they will be so difficult that you'll ask yourself why you got into this enterprise in the first place.

But there is good news: building a sustainable, thriving youth ministry is not only possible, it's actually predictable. Sadly, most churches don't have the patience to wait to build a sustainable youth ministry, so they opt for the roll of the dice.

FROM GAMBLING TO INVESTING

Heroic attempts at building immediate, inflated youth ministries almost never work—at least not for the long haul. Anxious churches that expect (and often demand) youth ministry results in a fraction of the time it truly takes pay for it eventually. Though these churches may justify the expectations placed on their current youth ministries (and youth ministers) with words about how important the mission is, the expectation of immediate results herniates the ministry, rendering it *less* capable of achieving the desired results.

Gambling is a far cry from investing. Churches that have failed to build sustainable youth ministries typically spend all their resources on quick fixes. Those churches spend very little time or energy investing in the future of their youth ministries.

Before he started his job as youth pastor at Saddleback Community Church, Doug Fields, arguably the most widely respected youth worker in the country, told his senior pastor that it would take five years (five years!) before the church could expect to see fruit from the youth ministry he'd be leading. Fortunately for the rest of us, Rick Warren had the foresight to sign on a guy with a long-term plan rather than a flash in the pan.

Those who have actually done it—those who *have* built thriving youth ministries—are those who weren't afraid to let their churches know up front that they would never meet the add-water-and-stir expectations.

I can hear the question you may be asking already: "With all this focus on investing in the future, what do we do about our youth ministry in the meantime?"

Here's the best answer: "Stop gambling, start investing and, in the meantime, do the best you can."

In the chapters that follow, you'll read about churches that have tried it both ways. By the time you turn the final page, you'll not only be convinced it can be done, but you'll also be equipped with the tools you'll need to build a youth ministry that lasts for the long haul. You'll learn from churches that have taken clear, calm, deliberate steps that made their youth ministries incrementally better, until one day, years later, the incremental investments produced exponential results.

First, we'll look at the "anatomy of stuckness" and identify the convergence of factors that keep churches chronically mired in lousy youth ministries.

Next, we'll talk through a whole new way of thinking about youth ministry, a way that pays attention to systems, structure and climate more than to tasks and great ideas.

Third, we'll focus on building a sustainable team to lead your ministry. You may be surprised by the discoveries we've made about the staff configuration found in the most effective youth ministries. We'll look at the most common hiring mistakes churches make in youth ministry and will identify the most explosive landmines youth workers step on (and how to avoid them).

Finally, we'll propose solutions to youth ministry's chronic and persistent challenges.

Real-life examples from churches and youth leaders we've worked with pepper this book. But often, because of the sensitive nature of an example or because a particular example might paint a certain church or leader in an unflattering light, we've chosen to jumble the details of some stories. Although the details may be different, the essential principles embedded in them will remain.

A WORD TO SENIOR PASTORS

As hard as it may be for you to believe, no one will influence the building of a sustainable youth ministry at your church like you will. In a survey of ten thousand Christian teenagers, kids rated only two qualities of church as more important than "a senior pastor who understands and loves teenagers." In other words, students said that the senior pastor has more influence on their choice of church than even their youth director. There's no one we'd rather have reading this book than you.

The fact that you've gotten this far suggests that you have more than a passing interest in the next generation. You are positioned to help your church see the importance of building your youth ministry slowly. You can instill patience as the church deliberately builds a youth ministry that lasts. And you can support your youth pastor when he or she is overwhelmed with criticism and broken on the sharp rocks of expectations that simply can't be met . . . at least this year anyway.

Extraordinary books and conventions are available to help youth workers and churches think theologically about youth ministry, resources that are helping us reimagine how youth ministry might look in this new millennium. But in spite of this growing number of excellent resources, our work with churches and youth workers has revealed an obvious gap between concept and reality, between theory and results.

> **The cycle of dysfunctional relationships between senior pastors and youth pastors must be broken. Youth pastors must learn how to commit themselves to uniquely prioritizing this relationship.**
>
> **RON KING**

With a dizzying array of statistics about how different kids today are or how the ways we've been doing ministry don't work anymore, senior pastors need a resource that gives them a picture of what *is* reasonable to expect from professional youth staff.

Many of our senior pastor friends have asked for help in leading their congregations through the difficult transition from a gambling approach to a sustainable approach in youth ministry. We offer this book as a youth ministry handbook for senior pastors and senior church leaders who may or may not have hands-on responsibility for the week-to-week management of ministry to teenagers.

A WORD TO SEARCH COMMITTEES

We hope that after you read chapters three and seven, you'll be convinced of these two bits of advice we often give to people in your position:

Don't hurry.
Don't settle.

Our recommendations are not terribly unlike the short and simple (but far from easy) advice from the book of Proverbs about marriage: "Don't marry the wrong one" (my paraphrase).

We've seen churches living in the aftermath of youth pastors whose hearts and motivation for ministry left years before they did. Another church decided that having no one in the youth director position would be better than having the current director. And other churches simply got tired of searching and decided to hire the person they all admitted was the best of all the mismatched candidates they'd looked at.

We trust your church will make different decisions.

A WORD TO YOUTH WORKERS

In some ways, then, this is a very different youth ministry book; most others are written almost exclusively to youth workers, with the unspoken assumption that the hired staff person *alone* holds the key to building a thriving youth ministry. But this book invites ordinary church leaders to build exceptional youth ministries without depending on short-term, superstar staff.

So if you have stepped into your current ministry with the dream that you'll take the church by storm and build the ministry you've dreamed of in six months, I beg you to reconsider.

Of course, it will be bad if you fail. But it could be worse—far worse—if you succeed. Though youth and parents might remember the glory days of your tenure on staff, there's a good chance you'll wind up like so many youth ministry superheroes, who leave gargantuan carnage in the wake of their one-of-a-kind, never-to-be-forgotten, it-will-never-be-as-good-as-it-was-back-then ministries.

The short-term, high-number, razzle-dazzle success of your current youth ministry might blind you to the fact that success in youth ministry is measured in decades, not in year-to-date comparisons with last year's mediocre youth staffer who, quite honestly, just didn't have your gifts.

So if you're hoping for a silver-bullet solution that describes *the* way Jesus did youth ministry, you'll have to look somewhere else. If you're hoping to be comforted and coddled in your frustration with your senior pastor, your difficulty in recruiting volunteers, or your inability to find time actually to be with Jesus or kids, you don't want this book.

But if you're sold on the idea of building a youth ministry that will be stronger years after you are gone than it is today, these hours we'll spend together will be well worth the investment.

WHY I'M EMBARRASSED BY THIS BOOK

The apostle Paul reminds us, "We have this treasure in jars of clay to show that this all-surpassing power is from God and not from us" (2 Cor 4:7). I'm embarrassed that this book is less about the treasure and more about the clay pots that carry the treasure. This book has grown out of the gaping hole in the competency of youth workers, who may know the treasure well but seem to have little capacity to carry it.

I'm making the assumption that your heart beats a little faster at the thought of seeing young people live into the dreams God has for them, growing into fully devoted disciples of Jesus Christ. That dream is, of course, where the real treasure is.

So this book is not a replacement for the marvelous, provocative works about the "treasure" that matters most in ministry, books like *Contemplative Youth Ministry, The Godbearing Life, Presence-Centered Youth Ministry* and *Jesus-Centered Youth Ministry*. These books insistently invite us into more Christ-centered, Spirit-driven ways of thinking about working with teenagers, pushing us beyond the activity-centered, anxiety-driven approach that has become part and parcel of today's youth ministry.

Despite the fact that more and more youth workers are thinking more theologically about doing ministry, those same youth workers find themselves stepping on the same landmines that have sidelined thousands of youth ministries before them. With so many extraordinary resources available, churches really don't need more ideas, more passion, more zeal, more energy, more enthusiasm. What they need is the ability to take what they already have and turn it into something that works.

But first we'll have to put away our infatuation with gambling.

1

CRACKING THE CODE

The Anatomy of Stuckness in Youth Ministry

The declining church always assumes that the solution to youth ministry is programmatic. If only they could get a good leader! If only they could find a great curriculum! If only they could renovate a room in the building for youth meetings! They fail to recognize that the solutions to youth ministry, like the solution to decline in general, is systemic.

THOMAS G. BANDY

He had done youth ministry earlier in his career, and quite successfully, he was quick to add. But over the past twenty years as a senior pastor, he had not once been able to establish a sustainable youth program in any church he'd served.

There were highlights, yes: a mission trip here, a particularly effective volunteer there and even a flash of success from a memorable, short-term youth director. But the only consistent thing had been his frustration.

After an exhaustive search and the hiring of yet another youth director (the one everyone had hoped would *finally* turn things around), it was soon all too obvious that a snowflake in the Sahara stood a better chance than this youth pastor's "new and improved" program.

That's when the call came.

The despair in the pastor's voice was anything but subtle. He was weary of following one new idea after another, hiring one new youth director after another. He was tired of unhappy parents of teenagers (he, in fact, was one of them), who couldn't understand why the church couldn't crack the code for building an effective youth ministry. He was tired of his youth ministry being compared (often disparagingly) to the church across the street. And he could no longer believe that this less-than-stellar ministry could all be blamed on busy kids, apathetic parents and hard-to-find volunteers. He was, in a word, *stuck*.

When a youth ministry isn't working, easy answers abound, the most popular of which is simply to "hire away" a church's youth ministry problems. But youth directors hired to save the day often find it difficult (if not impossible) to live up to the expectations they face from the first day they walk into their offices. And as flattering as it may be initially to be branded as "the answer," such an approach places on a youth worker a weight that few are called or equipped to carry.

As a result, most professional youth workers move on prematurely, some finding positions in other churches. But far too many, like one youth director we heard from recently, leave the land of youth ministry defeated and determined never to return. He wrote,

> I submitted my resignation as youth pastor yesterday. I can no longer continue in youth ministry or for that matter any ministry. I'm not sure if it was the overwhelming sense of failure or God's call. I sure hope it's the latter. So I am looking for a new job, not in ministry. Anyway, thanks for your time, but I don't see that it would make that much sense now.

The tragedy is that it doesn't have to be this way. Building a sustainable youth ministry is not a matter of getting lucky; there is no secret code to be cracked by the elite few. No, effective youth ministry happens when a very consistent set of factors is put in place, and it flounders when those factors are absent.

For me, the story of learning to move beyond stuck began the way most good stories begin—with a little drama.

THE NASHVILLE DRAMA

In 1986, I came to First Presbyterian Church in Nashville after working for eight years both in a church setting and in Young Life. Having experienced moderate "success" in my two previous ministries and having won my seminary's youth ministry award at graduation, I assumed that the Nashville ministry would be off and running like wildfire in no time. And I was not alone. I could smell the church leaders' enthusiasm as I stepped onto the scene, the answer to their prayers.

But after five years, I had clearly become more of a prayer request than a prayer answered. Despite my seventy-hour-plus workweeks, there were few visible signs that any progress had been made. Only a fraction of the youth of our church were active in the youth program. I simply couldn't break the code.

I prayed. I went to seminars. I read books. I prayed some more. I tried a variety of models, many of which described themselves as *the* biblical model for youth ministry. But nothing seemed to shake the inertia. We were stuck.

With nothing working, I made the unpopular decision to cancel youth group. It was clear that the way we were doing youth group simply wasn't working. So we stopped meeting every week and focused instead on creating periodic events, specifically targeting smaller groups. The idea seemed logical to everyone; everyone, that is, except the senior pastor, the youth, the parents and the elders.

A year and a half after the change, participation was increasing almost imperceptibly. I began talking more and more about an idea called family-based youth ministry, my first shot at building a sustainable foundation for youth ministry. But dramatic change didn't come until the storm hit.

We were having an ordinary, garden-variety youth committee meeting—at least I thought so. When I walked into the room, it was packed with twenty extra parents (mostly uninvited), all of whom had their opinion about what was wrong with the youth ministry, and for the next three hours, this group vented their feelings, an experience I now refer to affectionately as Rotisserie DeVries.

The next morning as I sat in my office, flipping through the want ads, fantasizing about how much easier it might be to sell cars, I got the call from Jim Robers, a busy, young businessman in our church. I certainly knew Jim's lively junior-high twin boys and his uber-volunteer wife much better than I knew him. He'd been at the meeting the night before. I braced myself for another round, knowing that our church had no rule against piling on.

His first words came out of left field. "That meeting last night . . . I realized about thirty minutes into it that you hadn't invited us there. I realized I'd been set up. I don't like being set up."

I was quiet, wondering where in the world this was going.

He continued, "I just want you to know that if there is anything, anything I can do for you as you try to build this program, I want to do it."

Not exactly knowing how he could help, I took him up on his offer, starting just by meeting him regularly for lunch. For the next six months, Jim, without even trying, taught me many of the core principles you will find in this book. Though he clearly didn't *have* time, he spent more time on lunches, phone calls and weekly committee meetings than either of us care to count.

Jim taught me what he knew: how to build an organization that works, how to build the "jars of clay" that can carry the treasure of the gospel. And as I ran behind Jim's blocks (as this elder in the church defended me again and again), I grew in confidence. But, more important, the youth ministry fundamentally changed, setting us on course to increase dramatically both our capacity and the quality of our work with students.

It is Jim's building principles that we'll be investigating in the coming chapters. But before we think about starting to build, we'll need to clear the site, removing the ideas and assumptions that most often get in the way of building on a solid foundation. We first need to identify the patterns that keep youth ministries stuck.

YOU KNOW YOU'RE STUCK IF . . .

Youth Ministry Architects has now assessed enough different kinds of youth ministries to recognize patterns and attitudes that keep so many youth ministries stuck. Together these attitudes make up what we have come to call the "anatomy of stuckness."

The typical stuck youth ministry is built on a number of unspoken assumptions, assumptions so woven into the fabric of youth ministry that they're barely discernible to the average youth worker. I'll put these assumptions in the form of five questions most commonly asked by stuck churches, questions that reveal fundamental misunderstandings that keep youth ministries from moving forward strategically.

Stuck question 1: Can you just give us some good ideas? I'll never forget my first youth workers convention. We stayed at the swankiest hotel I'd ever been in. I missed nothing . . . seminars on games, seminars on music, seminars on how to lead seminars.

I took incredible notes. I came home with one thing more than anything else: ideas. Our church actually ordered the entire set of *Ideas* books, certain that if we could just figure out the next great *idea,* we could make our ministry take off.

But it didn't take long to realize that few, if any, of those ideas translated into sustainable practices that

> For every problem, there is a solution which is simple, neat and wrong.
>
> H. L. MENCKEN

moved our ministry forward. I finally realized that I didn't need to go to a convention to get ideas: my church was full of them. In fact, some days it seemed everyone had *the* great idea that promised to move our ministry "to the next level."

In the stuck youth ministries we've observed, great ideas are legion. In focus groups, competing ideas are offered with such passion and enthusiasm that it's clear the speakers believe that the secret to a thriving ministry lies in trying this or that idea. Hang around struggling youth ministries long enough, and you'll be sure to hear much of what we have:

- We just need parents who are committed to the program (that is, who force their kids to come).

- We just need a pastor who really understands youth ministry.

- We just need to do it like Young Life does it.

- We just need a gym.

- We just need better couches in the youth room.

- We just need more contemporary music.

- We just need better theology.

- We just need more bowling.

- And (my personal favorite), we just need more cute boys and cute girls.

But fragmented collections of great ideas almost never work, particularly when the implementation of great ideas depends on some mythical "you" who is supposed to take responsibility for turning those ideas into reality. Until structures are in place for great ideas to be implemented, even the best of them will wind up on a treadmill that may speed up or slow down but will go nowhere.

Stuck question 2: *Can you keep us from failing?* Too many churches become paralyzed by their fear of having a failing youth ministry. But, as absurd as it may sound, it is often our *successes* that keep us stuck rather than our failures. Here's how:

Almost every church has *something* it has done in youth ministry that has "worked," perhaps an annual beach retreat, a favorite service project or a memorable musical tradition. Many focus obsessively on getting back to the success they once experienced.

But this journey in reverse (or, at best, in neutral) seldom leads out of the cesspool of dissatisfaction. If a ministry isn't working, it makes little sense to pour increasingly more energy into any single program, no matter how great a track record it might have had. A ministry that chooses to see its future only in the light of what has been will always stay stuck.

When we began our assessment at Anderson Community Church, people in almost every focus group spoke in glowing terms about the home-repair ministry that a youth director had launched more than ten years earlier. Upon probing, we learned that very few of the youth were engaged in this ministry at any level, though there were a number of committed adults. Yet many in our focus groups seemed absolutely certain that if the youth group could just get back to that single successful program, all would be well (and peace would return to Pride Rock).

Nothing characterizes successful organizations more than their willingness to abandon what made them successful.

MIKE WOODRUFF

Curious as it may be, few things keep churches more stuck than their successes. Here's the irony: Sustainable youth ministries fail all the time; they thrive in a culture of experimentation, innovation and creativity. It is floundering youth ministries that often remain paralyzed, unable to risk, stuck in a nostalgic obsession with past success.

Stuck question 3: Do you understand how different we are? Almost every church we have worked with suffered from a perception disorder we call "terminal uniqueness." In these churches, focus group members return again and again to the "unique" reasons for their less-than-thriving ministry, such as

- multiple high schools and middle schools, making it difficult for kids to feel connected

- youth with packed schedules, making many unable to participate regularly

- youth attending schools that demand high levels of performance, including multiple hours of homework every night

- potential volunteers who don't volunteer, leaving the staff to do almost everything

None of these challenges is even remotely unique to any one youth ministry. In fact, some combination of these factors has been present in every church we've worked with and in almost every effective youth ministry. A church that wants to avoid falling victim to the trap of terminal uniqueness will keep off the dead-end street of explaining away its less-than-effective youth ministry with these excuses.

Stuck question 4: Will you help my church understand that youth ministry isn't about numbers? Few principles are more sacred in youth ministry than this tired refrain (typically uttered with an air of absolute authority): "It's not about numbers."

We count what we believe to be important and whatever we count becomes important.

LYLE SCHALLER

We count people because people count.

WAYNE RICE

Conventional wisdom has it that talking about numbers is unspiritual and clearly antithetical to faithful ministry. But both the research and our experience reveal that numbers do, in fact, matter.

Youth Ministry That Transforms, the first thorough study of the profession of youth ministry, discovered surprisingly that "the size of a congregation's youth group is the greatest predictor of its overall climate." In addition, the study revealed a direct correlation between the number of youth and volunteers in a youth ministry and the "sense of team" experienced by the youth ministry as a whole. After decades of experience, Jim Burns and Mike DeVries (he is my brother in Christ, but no relation) summed it up clearly: "Youth go where the numbers are."

Anti-numbers churches remain stuck because they fail to recognize that students are drawn to places where there is at least a critical mass of youth, a place where they don't feel uncomfortably alone. To the average teenager, a room with "nobody there" is far less inviting than a room packed with friends and energy.

I know, I know. You may be ready to jump out of your skin right now. Let me qualify:

- A bigger youth ministry does not necessarily mean a better one.

- People in ministry do have a self-defeating and sometimes vicious habit of measuring their self-worth (and that of others) based on the size of their ministry.

- Some of the most important stuff of youth ministry doesn't happen in large groups but in one-on-one conversations and small groups.

But some numbers in youth ministry do matter, and matter profoundly. Consider this parable (borrowed from Rick Warren):

Imagine that Susan and I decide to take our teenage children to Disney World. As we send them off in the morning, we say, "We'll meet back here at the flagpole at 9:00 p.m." The children nod in agreement and run to the rides.

Nine o'clock comes, and Susan and I are at the flagpole. Debbie has arrived. Leigh has arrived. But Adam is nowhere to be found.

I look at my watch one more time and say to Susan, "Okay, honey, let's go."

Susan says predictably, "We can't go! Adam's not here."

I answer, "Listen, honey, Adam knew good and well what time we were meeting, and he's not here. We have two high-quality children here. Let's just work with the ones we've got. Let's go."

But my bride is immovable. She says, "Have you forgotten that we have three children?"

To which I respond, "Why are you so obsessed with numbers?!"

"Because that third one," she says, "just happens to be *ours*."

A church that doesn't determine how many students are a part of its youth ministry is irresponsible, just as a shepherd who fails to take the time to know how many sheep are in the flock would clearly be less than faithful in his or her charge. Likewise, a church that fails to determine how many students it would like to have involved on a weekly basis sets itself up for the anemia that comes from terminally vague expectations. If the target number is five students, the youth worker has clear marching orders.

Make no mistake about it. Every youth ministry *will* be evaluated by numbers. This evaluation may take place in a formal setting such as an elders meeting ("How many kids are we averaging in Sunday school?"). But more often, it takes place among a group of parents in the parking lot, at a party or on the phone, with conversations like this:

"My son says that no one comes any more."
"You know, my daughter says the same thing."
"All the kids are going to that church down the street."
"I wonder what our youth director is missing?"
"Well, if you want to know what I think . . ."

The question is not whether your youth ministry will be evaluated by numbers but whether the ministry will be evaluated by good numbers or bad numbers. Here are a few examples to show the distinction:

- Good number: How many students are "ours"?

- Bad number: How many youth are active at the Thursday morning breakfast at the popular church down the street?

- Good number: How many adult leaders do we need to provide enough capacity for all the kids who are "ours"?

- Bad number: Do we have more kids coming this year than last year?

- Good number: How many students do we want to have active on a weekly basis in our youth ministry?

- Bad number: How many different Sunday school classes do we offer?

- Good number: How many contacts have we made with visitors and inactive youth in the past month?

- Bad number: How many visitors did our youth group used to have in the glory days?

I hope you hear me. My beef is not that youth groups are too small (though most are much smaller than they should be). My beef is that churches often don't do the hard work of deciding what size youth ministry they'd like to have.

Having one foot on the accelerator and one foot on the brake doesn't work in driving, and it doesn't work in youth ministry. We can't say, "We don't care about numbers," and at the same time seek to grow our youth group.

> Whatever we measure really is our mission.
>
> RANDY FRAZEE

Stuck question 5: Can you get me out of all these political games? Too many youth workers proudly announce, "I don't play politics," and then wonder why they find themselves stymied by political battles over ministry minutiae. These youth workers are confused. They *are* playing politics; they're just playing poorly.

Perhaps a little reframing would help. When you think *politics,* think of the word's etymological cousin, *polite.* Learning to "play politics" well starts with simply doing the polite thing.

In a recent *Wall Street Journal* article on why top executives fail, "the inability to work with others" topped the list. Many of the executives left their positions with the complaint, "It was all about politics." But when probed further about what was meant by the word *politics,* the definitions boiled down to a single word: *relationships.*

Perhaps an example from my failure files would add a little clarity.

As he was repeatedly ambushed with youth ministry questions at social gatherings and church meetings, my senior pastor became increasingly distrustful of what I was doing. He approached me, carrying a powder keg of frustration, which was natural, considering all those surprise attacks directed at him that came because of something I did (or more often, didn't do). He called me into his office and said, "I need to know what's going on in the youth ministry!"

My response was neither polite nor politically wise. I said, "You never *ask* me about the youth ministry. Ask me anything you want to know, and I'll tell you." I failed to recognize that senior pastors are a lot like horses. They just don't do well when surprised.

The polite thing would have been for me to prepare him for the criticisms of the youth ministry he could expect and to arm him with reasonable responses to those attacks. Instead, I only increased his distrust of my judgment (and therefore the tension of my own work environment) because I didn't know how to "play politics." Understandably, the next time I went to him with a request that was a little out of the ordinary, like for an additional intern or permission to miss an elders meeting, his negative response was well deserved.

Most young youth workers step into ministry ill-equipped to walk through the political minefields that are a part of every church. Instead of recognizing that they need training in how the game is played, too many become unnecessary casualties in a battle they didn't even know they had signed up for.

By joining a church staff, a youth worker automatically steps onto the political playing field. And the one who holds firmly to "I don't play politics" often leads a ministry that is dramatically underfunded.

There may just be a connection.

BACK TO OUR STORY

What happened to our stuck senior pastor at the beginning of this chapter?

With a little help, he let go of his assumptions and stopped asking the questions that were keeping his youth ministry stuck. He walked through the processes you'll be reading about in the chapters to come.

He's not stuck anymore.

2

THE EASY BUTTON

The Crisis of Chronic Underinvestment

The history of primarily calling inexperienced and inadequately trained young people to do youth ministry reflects the myth that youth ministry is a beginner's job that doesn't require much education, experience or skill. Nothing could be farther from the truth. Youth ministry is one of the most demanding ministries—so demanding and frustrating that many pastors and congregational leaders don't know what to do.

ROLAND MARTINSON

Chatting over coffee at a convention a few years back, I met an animated young attendee. As he talked about his ministry, he voiced his long-standing frustration. Unable to grow, stuck in patterns that no longer seemed to work, the church had gone stagnant. "But," my new young friend explained, "after this week, everything will change."

"Really?" I asked. "How's that?"

He looked at me quizzically. "Why, this convention! I've brought my entire team here." He truly believed that "this convention," led by some of the most high-profile and engaging megachurch experts in the country, would immediately transform his stuck ministry into a thriving one.

Although I have little doubt that this young man's heart was in the right place, he had fallen victim to one of the most common, most crip-

pling myths about youth ministry: the Easy Button. Here are examples
of a few Easy Buttons:

- "All we need is one of those edgy worship services."

- "Now that we've found the biblical model for youth ministry . . ."

- "We've got to change our focus from programs to relationships."

Easy Buttons don't work in life; they don't work in marriage, and they
certainly don't work in youth ministry. Churches that try to build Easy
Button youth ministries find themselves just as stuck a decade from now
as they are today. Effective, sustainable youth ministries are found in
churches that give up the search for easy answers and, to borrow from
Eugene Peterson, practice "a long obedience in the same direction."

STEEPLE CHASE

Every now and then, when leading a youth ministry seminar, I try a
little exercise I call the Steeple Chase. Here's how it goes:

I ask the group how many of them come from churches that have steeples. Typically about half raise their hands. Then I ask, "Suppose that tonight the steeple were to be blown off your church. What would happen?"

Within a few seconds, someone shouts, "We would get it fixed!"

"But," I ask, "what if it was going to be *really expensive* to fix?"

"We'd still get it fixed," someone answers.

I keep pushing. "But what if getting the steeple fixed was going to be
a gargantuan hassle? What if the church just didn't have the money?"

By this point, the annoyed group responds with increased volume
and decreased speed, "We would *get it fixed!*"

When I ask how, the answer is almost always the same: "We would
figure it out."

Churches seem to know how to find the money to repair steeples,
don't they? Raising money to fix the HVAC system seems reasonable,
doable, just a natural part of being the church. Need a roof repaired? It
may be an annoying interruption, but most churches figure out how to
fund it.

Isn't it interesting how few churches feel anything close to this kind of urgency about their own youth, not to mention the thousands of disconnected youth in their community? Though youth ministry may be highly valued by most churches and though it has had little across-the-board success, churches often fail to see the need to invest appropriately in youth ministry.

It's time to acknowledge that our culture has dramatically underinvested in the creation of nurturing structures for its young and that churches have been among the slowest to invest. Several years ago I spoke to a group of parents at a church across town. They'd asked me to give a presentation about how their church might turn their chronically underperforming youth ministry into a thriving one. I could see in their eyes the familiar longing for the Easy Button.

As I taught, I explained that the difference between an effective and an ineffective youth ministry is often directly tied to the level of investment a church makes. I drew a line down the middle of the board. On the top of one column, I wrote the amount of financial investment our church was making in its youth ministry at that time. At the top of the other column, I wrote the amount this church was investing in its youth ministry. The first figure was ten times larger than the second.

"Could it be," I wondered aloud, "that the reason your church has chronically struggled in its youth ministry is tied less to the programs you're doing and more to the investment the church is making?" The parents nodded in agreement.

I was sure they were getting it; sure, that is, until one raised her hand. "I understand what you are saying about investment" (it would soon be clear that she had no idea what I was saying), "but give us some ideas about some of the neat programs that you do to get kids to come. I hear my kids talking about your ski trip and other things you do . . ."

A quick survey of the landscape of youth ministry reveals one disappointingly consistent result of underinvestment: youth ministry is undeniably in trouble. Consider these markers:

- "More than half of adolescents who attend church as children leave the church before they reach age seventeen."

- In one longitudinal study, 48 percent of adults confirmed in the Presbyterian Church left the church once they reached adulthood.

- "More than seven out of ten teens are engaged in some church-related effort in a typical week. When asked to estimate the likelihood that they will continue to participate in church life once they are living on their own, levels dip precipitously, to only one out of every three teens."

- "In a typical week, just three out of 10 twentysomethings attend church. Only 30% of adults in their 20's donated something to the church during the past year; the same percentage holds true for those who have read the Bible during any given week."

- From high school graduation to age 25, weekly church attendance drops 42 percent. It declines 58 percent from age 18 to age 29.

Louie Giglio's battle cry invites an investment at an entirely different level: "We're debating about whether to have carpet in the emergency room, while there are people bleeding to death all around us."

UNDERINVESTMENT: ALL TOO NORMAL

I've developed a theory about why youth ministry is so consistently underfunded: the short tenure, age and inexperience of most youth workers positions them to be ill-equipped to advocate for the level of investment necessary to build a sustainable youth ministry.

Consider this scenario: It's budget planning time again. The church's youth ministry, with a total budget of forty thousand dollars (including staff and programming), is engaging seventy-five youth each week. Jack, an affable twenty-four-year-old, leads the ministry in his first job out of college. Everyone likes Jack, but they see him as a kid himself.

The music program of the church, on the other hand, is led by Sandra, a fifty-three-year-old, dearly loved music minister who has been on the staff for more than twenty years. The music budget has grown to $120,000 a year.

When these two step into their respective meetings with the finance committee, one staff person has twenty-plus years of experience making church budget requests; the other has just one. If Jack is normal, he'll spend much more time grumbling about how small his youth ministry budget is than he will working the predictable processes most likely to ensure an adequately funded youth ministry.

I hope you hear me here. I am not suggesting that there's anything sinister about what the music staff person is doing. In fact, she's doing exactly what Jack *should* be doing: clearly and compellingly communicating her ministry's needs to the church. But Jack doesn't know how. He's choosing (yes, *choosing*) to do nothing to learn to become an expert in the complex process of successfully advocating for additional funding.

If Jack and Sandra's church is typical, Jack will be leaving in just a few years, handing an even less-experienced rookie the responsibility of advocating for funding. The very rhythm of youth ministry staffing in most churches almost guarantees that chronic underinvestment will be the norm.

(If, after hearing Jack's story, you're panicking about how in the world you'll be able to become successful at advocating for additional funding for your ministry, skip ahead to chapter twelve, "Dancing with Alligators.")

MIS-INVESTMENT: IT LOOKS SO GOOD

When I walked into St. John's Church on the first day of the assessment, I was impressed. The youth facilities were state of the art. There was a gymnasium, a fully equipped rec room and an inviting collection of comfortable couches. But after a few focus groups, I could tell that this was a ministry in trouble.

It seems that the church had raised two million dollars to build facilities for youth, but had absolutely no plans for increasing the staff for the youth ministry. As a result, for the past six months, the lone staff person had doubled (or should we say "divided"?) as a facilities manager/recreation director, overseeing a complex and demanding basketball league, leaving even less time for his already overloaded plate as youth director. As you might imagine, at the time of this writing, the church is looking for a new youth minister, again.

Too many churches make this classic mis-investment blunder. Let's imagine another way the two million might have been used. If they'd taken that money and invested it at a rate of 5 percent, they would have been able to hire two or three additional full-time youth staff for decades, without ever tapping into the principle. Great buildings seldom precede great youth ministries.

More times than we would like to count, we've come to "edifically obsessed" churches that have chosen to make the vast majority of their youth ministry investment in buildings. But gymnasiums, air-hockey tables, plasma TVs and leather couches don't build thriving youth ministries; appropriate staffing, clear vision and structure do. Too many churches are like parents spending thousands on a playroom for their children while neglecting the kids' need for food and clothes, assuming that the fortune they have already spent on their kids should be enough.

I've been known to make people mad. (Not often, fortunately.) The one issue that makes people the angriest is the cost and how long it takes to get a sustainable youth ministry up and running. Most churches want their youth ministry fixed fast and cheap. Though we can usually stop the bleeding quickly, restoring the "body" back to health takes a much longer time.

We understand the pressure people feel to build quickly:

- "We have all these juniors and seniors, and if we don't get this thing fixed now, we're going to lose them."

- "Our kids are worth it. They deserve better than this."

- "We can't afford to wait."

Good arguments, all of them, but none is an excuse for avoiding building structures of sustainable youth ministry.

Churches build buildings because the cost is clear; architects can give a good estimate of what it will take. But churches have a much harder time determining what it costs to build a sustainable youth ministry.

THE CRISIS OF CAPACITY

One characteristic shared by many churches we work with is "the crisis of capacity." Churches that suffer under this crisis are like

- a driver trying to carry five thousand pounds on a cart built for one thousand pounds (eventually the cart will buckle under the weight)

- a captain loading a lifeboat designed for twenty-five with one hundred people (if all the passengers can even get on, the boat will sink)

- a child trying to stay warm with a two-by-two-foot blanket (resulting in coldness and irritation)

Often, crisis-of-capacity churches contact us because they're frustrated by the chronic "underperformance" of their youth workers. Balls are getting dropped. Parents are frustrated by the lack of information they receive. The senior pastor is tired of the youth ministry being the hot button in the church.

But often we find that the apparent "failure" of the youth ministry is caused less by an underperforming youth worker than by an overcapacity ministry. Assuming that a more

No good general ever started a battle that he hadn't already won.

CHINESE GENERAL SUN TZU

organized youth worker is needed (or a more relational one, or a more magnetic one, or . . .), overcapacity churches forget to ask the fundamental question of whether their performance expectations are even reasonable. In short, they ignore the question of capacity.

MEET THE NORMALS

Over the past five years, we've discovered five fairly consistent "normals" for understanding capacity in youth ministry. Though not all these normals are always present in every church, every church has had some clear combination of them.

1. One thousand to fifteen hundred dollars a kid. The most controversial of all the normals, this rule of thumb suggests that a church that expects to have one hundred youth involved on a weekly basis needs to have a budget in the neighborhood of $100,000, including the program budget, staff salaries and benefits. Though a change in staff or a change in youth ministry model may create a shift in *which* specific students a church engages, it's not likely that the youth ministry will be able to increase the net number of youth participating without an increase in funding. Ordinarily, overcapacity youth ministries result in short-term youth directors and programs that quickly launch and then sputter out of existence. We've certainly worked with churches that were spending more or less than this benchmark amount, but we've found it to be a very reasonable and dependable marker of just how much a sustainable youth ministry normally costs.

2. *One full-time staff person for every fifty youth.* According to this normal, a church that hopes to sustain the involvement of fifty youth on a weekly basis needs to hire the full-time equivalent of one staff person. When a church hires just enough staff to barely maintain the program they have and then expects quantum growth from the new hire, the understaffed youth ministry can be expected to remain mired in a climate of criticism, blaming and burnout. An overcapacity youth ministry sets up its staff and volunteers to be unable to fulfill the wide variety of expectations placed on them by the parents, the youth, the senior pastor and the church leaders.

3. *One adult for every five youth.* We like to think in terms of "spans of care," recognizing that, realistically, most volunteers can't effectively oversee the church's Christian nurture of more than about five students on an ongoing basis. A church seeking to build a youth ministry with twenty-five youth active weekly will need approximately five volunteers working weekly in the ministry. Conventional wisdom would suggest that if enough volunteers are in place, staff will be less necessary. But our experience is just the opposite. Without sufficient staff to coordinate, inspire and equip volunteers, the volunteers easily become stuck in competing priorities and programs that eventually erode the long-term sustainability of the ministry.

Though the first three normals can provide a congregation with a prescription for aligning their investment in youth ministry and their expectations, it's important to provide two more normals linking youth-group participation to the church's overall membership.

4. *Ten percent of the worshiping congregation.* In a typical church, the size of the youth ministry tends to settle at around 10 percent of the worshiping congregation. Unless it invests otherwise, it's likely that a church with an average worship attendance of five hundred will have about fifty students active in some way in the life of the church. At the same time, a church with a weekly worship attendance of five thousand might have a much larger youth group than the church's investment (in budget, staff and volunteers) might predict, with youth participation pulled along by high levels of participation in the larger church.

5. *A 20-percent ceiling.* We've observed that churches can naturally grow their youth ministries to a size equivalent to about 20 percent of the worshiping congregation simply by increasing their investment (see normals one to three, above) and moving forward for several years with a consistent structure and vision. But when the size of the youth ministry begins to exceed the 20-percent mark, the norms become much less predictable. In other words, a church with five hundred people participating in worship could naturally grow its youth ministry to one hundred simply by increasing its investment. But as the youth ministry seeks to grow beyond the one-hundred mark, increased investment alone will not necessarily increase the number of youth involved weekly.

> Growth and decline in youth ministry attendance is closely linked to the ups and downs of Sunday morning attendance. . . . Among the 460 churches represented in the survey, if worship attendance was up, so was youth group attendance. The opposite was also true. A decline in worship attendance generally meant youth group numbers would similarly sink.
>
> LEN KAGELER

A disclaimer: When we present these norms, we're often asked, "Where did you get these?" Our response is that, like a contractor who has built forty or fifty houses in the last few years, we're able to estimate a general "cost per square foot" with sometimes frightening accuracy.

But we also encourage church leaders to "do the math" for themselves and to analyze their current youth ministry using these metrics. Even if they come up with numbers and ratios different from ours, answering these questions will provide them with a clear sense of what it takes in their particular context to maintain the current youth ministry and offer a baseline for predicting the cost of strategic growth.

There are, of course, a few exceptions to these norms:

- Churches that have youth groups roughly the size of Jesus' youth group (twelve or so) can typically do youth ministry much less expensively.

- Youth groups in towns with only one junior high and high school sometimes find it possible to attract larger numbers of students than the norms might predict.

- At times the various norms can inversely impact each other. For example, one church may not have a thousand-dollar-a-kid budget, but its high staff and volunteer ratios can balance out its lack in financial investment. Another church might have almost no volunteers but make up for the lack by high levels of investment in staff. But like a beach ball pushed under water, most youth groups tend to return to equilibrium right around these norms.

St. Michael's Church, for example, determined that, given the number of youth connected to their church, they wanted to move from having 45 youth involved weekly to having 150. After years of gambling, placing their bets on the hope of finding just the right youth minister, just the right program or just the right promotion plan, they decided they would take the investment approach instead.

The first year, they hired a full-time youth program director to join the full-time youth director. The next year, multiple interns were added.

During the third year, a second full-time youth director replaced the multiple interns. At the same time, they dramatically increased the number of volunteers involved, moving from less than ten to more than thirty adults involved weekly. Within three years, their ministry was engaging well over one hundred

> **If you have a group of twelve kids who don't understand your illustrations and one of them wants to kill you, you have a youth group just like Jesus.**
>
> **MARK YACONELLI**

youth a week. Though still not at the one-to-fifty ratio, they're well on their way, having established a clear trajectory for growth, simply by intentionally increasing their investment and thus their capacity.

The extraordinary news is that the doomsday predictions are wrong. The epidemic of lament surrounding youth ministry, though a welcome wake-up call, may actually be misguided. Churches that move beyond gambling and choose to invest strategically, with an eye to the long-term investment, are seeing delightful and dramatic returns.

3

HOPING, WISHING AND PRAYING

Beyond the Frantic Search for the Youth Ministry Superstar

The pressure to succeed is especially acute for youth ministers, who—despite their lack of knowledge, skills and experience—are expected to attract young adolescents to a life of commitment to Christ and the church. It is a daunting task made increasingly difficult by the expectations of adults and a notable lack of congregational support.

MERTON STROMMEN

The request was one we'd heard often enough, but never this blatantly: "Can you help us find a superstar youth director?"

My response came so abruptly that it shocked even me. "That is one thing we just don't do."

After an awkward silence, I explained that after years of watching churches search for *and hire* "superstar" youth directors, I'd come to the conviction that helping churches find superstars doesn't really help. Instead of helping build long-term, sustainable youth ministries, the superstar orientation does just the opposite: it keeps youth ministries stuck.

I've grown weary of churches spending heroic, sacrificial energy (and money) trying to build quick-fix, big-win youth ministries, only to find themselves three years down the road with nothing to show for their efforts but overblown memories of a burned-out superstar.

It's easy enough to understand. Parents get worried about their kids; they get desperate, clawing at any shred of hope they can find. Churches exhibit a similar desperation when they find themselves on the verge of extinction because their kids are staying away in droves. And when we get desperate, we also get stupid.

At Youth Ministry Architects, we've seen the pattern enough times to no longer question its predictability. The story usually goes something like this . . .

FIRED, HIRED AND TIRED

You could almost see the heel marks all the way to the doors of the church. Jim Johnson's daughter, Annie, *hated* the youth program. She hated the dorky games; she hated the way the kids were so exclusive; and she really hated that her parents *made* her participate. So when Ryan was asked to leave his role as youth pastor, there were no tears shed at the Johnson house.

When the pastor called Jim to ask him to lead the search committee for a new youth director, Jim was thrilled. Quite honestly, in his estimation, Ryan had been a disappointment at best. It broke Jim's heart to pick up his daughter at church and hear her say, with her typical flare for the dramatic, "*Please* don't make me go back there, Dad. I would rather have a brain tumor than have to walk into that room again!"

So by the time Ryan had left town, Jim had filled his committee and the search had begun in full force. The committee (made up mostly of parents whose sons and daughters had been less-than-enthusiastic about Ryan's ministry) made their list of what they were looking for.

- Ryan's program had been too activity centered. The search committee wanted a youth director who could teach the Bible with substance and still keep kids' attention.

- Ryan had never had time to visit the kids at their schools like the previous youth pastor did; that would need to be a high priority.

- And Ryan simply couldn't draw a crowd. They wanted someone who was more outgoing, whose personality could attract kids to the ministry.

They put together a job description, and for six months, they made phone calls, conducted interviews and went to more meetings than any of them had expected. At the end of the six months, they had narrowed their search to three candidates.

Before long, they hired Andrew, an incredibly creative, relational, student-focused young man in his twenties with an apparently endless supply of energy. The search committee enjoyed his sense of humor immensely, and they were certain the kids would too.

But by the end of the first year, Andrew came to the unsettling realization that relating to students was only a fraction of what he was expected to do. The church also looked to him to recruit and train adult volunteers, select and gain approval for curriculum resources, organize major youth ministry events, keep up with all the money that came in for retreats and camps, relate to parents and businesspeople, and make peace between members of his team. In a word, he was expected to do the one thing he promised the search committee he was not good at: organize.

As details fell through the cracks left and right, criticism from parents and church leaders increased exponentially. Andrew began to realize that though he thought he was hired to *do* the work of the youth ministry, he was also expected to *build the structure* for the youth ministry. He felt like a mechanic charged with working on his car's engine while driving it down the highway at seventy miles an hour.

As the decibel level of complaints increases, we can only guess that Andrew will soon be looking for another position, very likely outside youth ministry and the church altogether. And that church will begin the search cycle all over again.

THE TELLTALE SIGNS OF A SUPERSTAR SEARCH

Even a cursory review of the number of churches searching for youth workers reveals the immense imbalance between the need and the availability of trained, effective youth workers. A glance at the typical job posting shows why.

Most youth pastor job postings suffer from chronic vagueness on the one hand and wildly unrealistic expectations on the other. Too often, youth pastors are set up to be judged as failures by at least one of their constituencies. Just for the sake of illustration (and morbid entertainment), I've pulled a few excerpts from ads of churches searching for youth workers. My comments are in parentheses.

- Build a dynamic, life-changing ministry to teens in our church and in the surrounding community. (Part-time!)

- Develop, coordinate and lead all aspects of youth ministry for middle and high school youth, and the college/careers young adult group. (In a church of three thousand, as the sole youth staff person.)

- Create a contemporary and relevant strategy [for our] youth ministry, . . . integrating personal prayer and study of God's Word, evangelism, fellowship, worship, discipleship, tithing and service, including long-range strategy, short-term goals and specific objectives toward implementing each goal. (How many forty-five-year-old senior pastors can do this?)

- Provide dynamic, visionary leadership for student ministries in grades 6 through 12. . . . Responsibilities include vision casting, leadership training, budget management, strategizing, and the planning and implementation of ministry programs. . . . Candidates should be high-level leaders, creative, passionate about students, energetic, hard working, team oriented, and able to motivate others. Candidates must have a minimum of 3 years relevant experience in youth ministry. The ability to communicate in Spanish would also be preferred. (Part-time!)

- Required skills: Excellent team-based leadership abilities; exceptional communication and organizational skills; understanding of student/ teen lifestyle issues and cultural trends; great relational skills with students and adults of all backgrounds and situations. (I want to meet this one!)

Too many churches are looking for a dynamic, top-notch, committed, magnetic, relational, creative, organized, theologically informed, twenty-two-year-old who can present powerful, life-changing messages and will gratefully work for $23,000 a year. The excruciatingly exaggerated requirements found in so many of these job descriptions gives evidence of little more than a history of chronic dissatisfaction with those who have gone before.

Consider the way most professions work. In sports, the number of rookies on the field at any given point in the game is almost always smaller than the number of experienced players. In medicine, law and business, though there are plenty of rookies, there are few successful organizations that put rookies *in charge* the day they arrive. In fact, even after they have a medical degree, physicians are required to serve a minimum of three years out of medical school under an experienced practitioner before being licensed to serve on their own.

Youth ministry may be one of the only professions that has settled into the pattern of handing over total responsibility for running an organization to young people just out of college. Far too often, anxiety, not wisdom, drives us.

TESTING YOUR CHURCH FOR THE SUPERSTAR VIRUS

How can a church know if it's working with a superstar mentality? Over the years, we've discovered five telltale statements from churches afflicted with the superstar virus. See if any of these comments sound familiar.

1. *"Our youth staff should know how to do it."* I remember well my first full-time youth ministry job. Just out of college, I was overwhelmed and over my head. My prayer life was doing fine. I was teaching well and building incredible relationships with students, but there were simply more plates to spin than I knew how to manage.

My youth ministry meetings were full of highly organized parents and adult volunteers. But I simply didn't know how to structure the ministry to access their immense organizational gifts. So, instead of carrying some of the administrative load of managing details of the youth ministry, they simply lobbed advice grenades from a distance.

I would leave those meetings with an even longer to-do list, frustrated that my "team" had delegated almost every responsibility back to me. Something was wrong with this picture: the only role these highly organized adults chose to play was to complain about my lack of organizational skills.

I was well into my third *decade* in youth ministry when I finally began to feel confident accessing the immense gifts of those who really wanted to help me. As a twenty-two-year-old, I didn't know enough to know what I didn't know. I assumed it was my volunteers' problem. I realize now that I was living out Ted Smith's powerful description of the shortsighted way churches handle the "problem" of youth ministry: "We delegate youth ministry to folks who are structurally the most vulnerable, thus preventing the youth ministry from ever challenging the church with the gospel."

Superstar-oriented churches assume that the "professional" youth worker should just *know* how to organize volunteers to share the workload, how to do the strategic thinking that will result in carloads of kids showing up. Those churches are almost always disappointed.

2. "Our youth worker will know the difference between wallpaper and concrete." In any construction project, there's a definite order that must be followed. For example, hanging sheetrock before running electricity through the house can more than double the amount of work required. If a builder tries to hang wallpaper before laying the cement foundation, there'll be nothing but a sticky mess.

In building a sustainable youth ministry, first things must come first. But because most of those responsible for building a youth ministry are building for only the first or second time, they build like children handed a stack of wood, a hammer and some nails. With no blueprint, they simply start nailing things together as quickly as possible, which works fine for a slap-together fort in the backyard, but won't result in a lasting structure.

Let's get a little more specific about how Wallpaper Before Concrete (or WBC) youth ministries look.

- WBC youth ministries spend weeks redecorating their youth room (wallpaper) before they have a calendar of events completed for the year (concrete).

- WBC youth ministers have time to check their email and their favorite websites in the morning (wallpaper), though they don't yet know the names of all the youth in their program (concrete).

- WBC youth ministries love to try out the latest youth ministry fads (wallpaper) before they recruit enough volunteers to ensure that every student in the program has at least one adult from the church in his or her life (concrete).

- WBC youth ministries hand responsibility over to the students (wallpaper) before they have developed clear, measurable goals consistent with where the church leaders would like to see the youth ministry go (concrete).

3. "Our new youth worker will bring an end to all these crises." It never ceases to amaze me how often youth workers and churches are surprised about problems in their youth ministry. To adapt the first line of Scott Peck's *The Road Less Traveled,* youth ministry "is difficult." It always is. It always will be.

- Volunteers don't line up and do exactly what we expect them to do.

- Not every parent appreciates our efforts (or our sense of humor).

- Kids do not automatically come to youth meetings just because a new, "cool" youth worker has been hired.

This much we know . . . or at least we should know.

Sooner or later, something always hits the fan. A friend of mine says that there are only two periods in any youth ministry: crisis and pre-crisis. It is what we do in the pre-crisis stage that will determine the long-term health of our ministry. Senior pastors do resign, churches face budget cuts, youth directors get mono, youth leaders have affairs, and innocent people get caught in political crossfire. Crises will come.

When a youth minister is expected to prevent crises from erupting, that person is set up for failure.

4. "We'll never hire from within our church." One of Jim Collins's surprising discoveries in his study of "good to great" companies was that, in over 90 percent of those companies (ten of eleven), the CEO was *not* a superstar savior hired from the outside but someone who had been a part of the company for a long time.

We've observed a similar phenomenon in youth ministries. Some of the most powerfully effective youth workers emerge from within the churches they've been serving. They step into their professional role with relationships and connections and with years of appreciation for the unique climate of the church.

The policy of not hiring church members almost always comes out of a negative experience that could have been prevented had clear accountability been in place before the hire-from-within took place. Trapped in a culture of niceness, most churches choose to create broad policies instead of dealing directly with those who are not fulfilling the expectations of their jobs.

Though hiring from within clearly carries risks, our experience has been that these risks are far smaller than those taken by churches gambling on a superstar outsider.

5. "With a new youth director, our volunteers won't have to work so hard." Finally, we have observed on superstar-focused search teams the debilitating expectation that the vast majority of the work volunteers have been doing heroically for months (sometimes years) will be lifted from their shoulders the day the new youth director steps into the office.

Do the math with me. Suppose ten people are each volunteering five hours a week, keeping the transitional youth ministry up and running. When the new youth director arrives (with a bandwidth of around fifty hours a week), he or she is

> In an organization, leaders must be brought from the outside. In a movement, leaders emerge from within.
>
> ERWIN McMANUS

immediately handed all the work the interim volunteers have been doing. The result is a net gain of exactly zero hours a week, and the youth director is left wondering why the new program can't seem to get traction. Add to this equation the extra duties of a staff person—weekly staff meetings and functions, multiple committee meetings, assisting in worship—and you can see why it's not unusual to add staff and actually move backward.

Do the Math

   50 hours per week of a new staff person

 - 10 hours of functions unrelated to youth ministry

 - 50 hours of previous volunteer help
_____

   10 fewer hours available for youth ministry

The five attitudes of superstar youth ministries all add up to what has become a very toxic culture for youth workers, many of whom leave youth ministry after their first overwhelming experience. A study conducted for the National Catholic Conference of Bishops confirms this hypothesis. While research revealed that the vast majority (over 90 percent) of parish ministers find their work very satisfying, the same report tells a quite different story about those serving as youth ministers:

> Of the various ministry positions, youth ministers seem to derive the least satisfaction and support. The full-time youth ministers find ministry the least affirming, their coworkers the least affirming, their supervisors the least satisfied, parishioners the least satisfied, and youth ministers the least likely to encourage others to enter parish ministry.

ONE MORE REASON WHY SUPERSTARS FAIL

Johnson Chapel Christian Church hired a superstar. They had wooed Jeff from his thriving ministry across the country, offering to let him "bring his own vision" to the youth program. If ever there was one, Jeff was a superstar. He had the whole package: experience, charisma, wisdom.

With twelve years of experience under his belt, Jeff was hired to serve as the youth pastor at a church with over five hundred youth on its rolls. It had been years since the church had had its last permanent youth director, and church leaders were sure that as soon as Jeff stepped on the scene, the vast majority of the youth they had "lost" during the interim would come back (apparently no one thought to consider that half of those youth had already graduated from high school and would never be "coming back" to the youth group).

After working for two years as the sole youth staff member, Jeff's group stood at a steady participation level of 250 active youth a week. But it had plateaued there. And before long, ideas and suggestions were flying toward him like projectiles at a substitute teacher.

Jeff was given well-meaning hints like, "Work smarter, not harder," and "Do the important things; not the urgent things," and the less-than-helpful "You need to slow down more." In the most blatant display of the superstar syndrome I've ever seen, the church sent Jeff to counseling to help him discover what

> Like a light bulb attracts bugs, we expect the youth pastor to attract kids. When the youth pastor burns out, the kids go away, and the search for a new bulb begins (along with the hope that this one will last just a little bit longer).
>
> WAYNE RICE AND
> MILES McPHERSON

his problem was, to find out exactly why he seemed so overwhelmed all the time. Forget the fact that the number of youth he was engaging weekly was easily in the top ten of any church in his denomination in the country. Forget that the church never took the time to find out how many churches had 250 active youth and one staff person. With blind certainty, the leaders of this church assumed that if there was a problem in this ministry, it couldn't be the superstar expectations of the system. It had to be the staff person.

Jeff is now in a new position with more reasonable expectations. The church has started another search. At least one of the parties is happy.

The superstar syndrome always creates larger problems, not the least of which is removing the family, the elders, the deacons and other concerned adults from the lives of teenagers and replacing them with a new "youth ghetto" in which the rest of the church simply lets the youth minister take care of the kids.

Superstar-syndrome churches spend sacrificial amounts of energy on the roller-coaster ride of gambling on the *next* youth pastor. But ironically, superstar youth ministries come from churches that spend their energy creating a climate and building an infrastructure in which moderately gifted, garden-variety youth directors produce superstar results.

4

THE DANCE FLOOR

A Systems Approach to Youth Ministry

It is unrealistic to expect to be able to design and implement an effective turnaround strategy without removing some of the systemic barriers to change.

LYLE SCHALLER

Leaders are responsible for both the big structures that serve as cornerstones of confidence, and for the human touches that shape a positive emotional climate to inspire and motivate people.

ROSABETH MOSS KANTER

Years of preparation had made her movements effortless, her turns seamless, her leaps weightless. A dancer of unparalleled talent, she mesmerized the crowd with her skill, but even more with her passion. Her countenance proclaimed in no uncertain terms that she was made for this moment.

But she would finish much sooner than anyone expected. Coming down from an arching leap, she landed with a jolting crack, her foot driving its way through the rotting wood of the floor, her body twisted in pain, her leg bent in places it was not made to bend. She was pulled from the stage, wondering if she would ever dance again.

The master of ceremonies dismissively apologized, "Inexperience does this to a dancer."

But no one repaired the floor.

And then, as if nothing had happened, the next performer was introduced. The crowd responded with a smattering of applause. But with no one attending to the dance floor, the audience knew that the new dancer would also find her performance ending prematurely with a disappointing, perhaps tragic, conclusion.

"Attending to the dance floor" may be the most neglected task in youth ministry. When the dance floor is in bad repair, talent is not enough. Right preparation is not enough. Not even passion and enthusiasm can prevent the inevitable dissatisfaction and disaster.

Failure to attend to the dance floor ensures that a toxic environment will infect the entire system, a system in which most, if not all, youth workers are likely to fail. The world of youth ministry today is filled with dancers of unparalleled talent who crash and burn, not because they can't dance, but because they and their churches know nothing about building and tending to dance floors.

What far too many churches and youth workers are missing is the ability to give their first attention

> **Simple church leaders are designers. . . . Complex church leaders are programmers. . . . Church leaders who are programmers focus on one program at a time. Their goal, though never stated, is to make each program the best. Church leaders who are designers are focused on the end result, the overall picture. They are as concerned with what happens between the programs as they are with the programs themselves.**
>
> THOM RAINER
> AND ERIC GEIGER

to ensuring that the right systems, priorities and infrastructure are in place before beginning the dance.

TAKING THE SYSTEMS APPROACH

In this chapter and the three that follow, I invite you into seeing (and doing) youth ministry with a systems perspective. More and more, we are discovering that sustainable youth ministries are led by systems leaders. The day of the camp counselor youth minister who focuses only on students is over. Sustainable youth ministries make the leap from a short-term, patchwork ministry to ones based on established systems that last long after the current leadership team has moved on.

Every church can build a sustainable youth ministry by attending first to the two key components of systems thinking in youth ministry:

1. Architecture: the structures of sustainability

2. Atmosphere: the culture, climate and ethos that sustain the health of an organization

I'll take the next two chapters to spell out how these components play out in a sustainable youth ministry. But first, I want to bring a little more clarity to this whole notion of a uniquely *systems* approach to youth ministry.

CONTENT THINKING VERSUS SYSTEMS THINKING

As I have tried to get my head around the power of a systems approach to initiating strategic change, family systems theory has been immensely helpful, particularly in its distinction between "content issues" and "system issues."

A content issue involves a specific topic, usually a topic of conflict. In youth ministry, typical content issues can be anything from a problem with cliques to a problem with the seventh-grade curriculum.

System issues, on the other hand, are those processes that take place beneath, around and within the particular topics of concern, things like *trust* among the leadership, *clarity* of expectations for staff and volunteers, or *ownership* of the ministry beyond the staff.

Trying to initiate change while staying solely focused on content issues is like sprinting up and down the aisle of a speeding jet, believing that the sheer force of effort will speed up the plane. Too many youth workers are wearing themselves out, completely unaware of the fact that they are a part of a system that is carrying them (and their ministries) in a direction that may be completely independent of their exhausting labor.

The hired youth staff person often becomes the content issue of choice when it's time for launching criticism at a youth ministry. "Simple" solutions to a youth ministry's problems almost always start with a focus on the youth director: he just needs to get organized; she just needs to get out of the office and spend more time with kids; he just needs a little more training; or (the more permanent solution) she just needs to *go*.

But dramatic, sustainable change happens in youth ministries only when we take our focus off the "presenting issues"—the obvious concerns that seem to be creating so much anxiousness—and put our focus on the system patterns that keep us locked into unproductive ways of doing things.

> When one part of [an] organism is treated in isolation from its interconnections with another, as though the problem were solely its own, fundamental change is not likely. The symptom is apt to recycle, in the same or different form, in the same or different member. Trying to cure a person in isolation from his or her family . . . is as misdirected, and ultimately ineffective, as transplanting a healthy organ into a body whose imbalanced chemistry will destroy the new one as it did the old. It is easy to forget that the same family of organs that rejects a transplant contributed to the originally diseased part becoming foreign.
>
> EDWIN FRIEDMAN

PAUL: THE SYSTEMS THINKER

Most of us who have grown up in the church know Paul's famous words to the Philippians, "Rejoice in the Lord always. I will say it again: Rejoice!" (Phil 4:4). We may have sung these words at camp or memorized them in Sunday school, but I'll bet few could describe the context in which these words were written.

They come right in the middle of Paul addressing two women in the church who just can't seem to get along. He writes, "I plead with Euodia and I plead with Syntyche to agree with each other in the Lord. Yes, and I ask you, loyal yokefellow, help these women who have contended at my side in the cause of the gospel" (Phil 4:2-3).

Instead of addressing the *topic* of the conflict (which Paul seems to purposely ignore), he takes a systems approach. He refuses to get sucked into a debate over the content issue plaguing this young church. Instead he makes a beeline to the process, the system surrounding that issue. His clear assumption is that only in the context of intentional, *chosen* joy will the Philippian church effectively move beyond the debilitating power of petty conflicts.

Youth ministry is not an event but a process.

BARRY ST. CLAIR

Ron was a new youth pastor with great ideas (ideas are almost always content focused). When he stepped into a youth ministry with less than 5 percent of the teenagers of the church participating regularly, he took the *Field of Dreams* approach: "If I build it, they will come." Well, Ron built it. He planned engaging events; he planned Bible studies; he planned opportunities for student leadership.

He built it. But they didn't come. He envisioned a gym full of students playing together, worshiping together, hearing an engaging message from Scripture together.

Great *idea*. But there were a few things missing: students, leaders and, most important, a system in place designed to deliver the results Ron longed to see. He needed more than hard work and a fragmented collection of great ideas. He needed the kind of systemic change that must be built deliberately over a course of years.

THE PROVERBS 14:4 CHALLENGE

As we embark on making the shift to a systems way of doing youth ministry, I invite you to take the Proverbs 14:4 Challenge. This obscure proverb has the power to reframe our understanding of the kind of hassle involved in building a sustainable ministry.

> Where there are no oxen, the manger is empty,
>> but from the strength of an ox comes an abundant harvest.
>> (Prov 14:4)

I know—it's not exactly a passage that will start a revival. But these words offer a clear challenge to any church still looking for the Easy Button. Let me put it in other words:

> If you want a manger free of ox poop, don't buy an ox.
> But if you want to multiply your harvest, an ox sure will come in handy.

The challenge of sustainable youth ministry is as straightforward as the proverb: Want to build a ministry that lasts, a ministry that deeply impacts students, families and the wider world? Then be prepared for the mess.

5

BUILDING RIGHT

The Structures of Sustainability

Your ministry is perfectly designed to achieve the results you are currently getting.

ANDY STANLEY

Be sure you know the condition of your flocks.

PROVERBS 27:23

The guru par excellence of church conflict always told me that the most important thing in working in a hot fight is to recognize that everybody wants to simplify the issues so you have clear reasons for killing each other. . . . He said that the most important thing one can do is to "complexify things." . . . When you see all ten sides of the issue you'd mistakenly thought had only two, only then can you begin working out of the polarization.

DIANA BUTLER BASS

From as early as the sixteenth century, rulers and merchants from around the world dreamed of finding a shorter route between the Atlantic and Pacific Oceans. If a canal on the Isthmus of Panama could be built, they imagined, the distance required to travel between the two oceans could be reduced to a fraction of the original trip.

But over the centuries, builders and engineers were thwarted again and again in their attempts to build a waterway across those forty-eight miles between the two oceans. A vast array of obstacles stood in their way, not the least of which was a sizable hill right in the middle of that stretch of land. The first builders attempted to simply plow through the mountain, in hopes of building a flat, sea-level-to-sea-level canal. After all, they assumed, it would be *impossible* to get a ship to travel uphill.

It wasn't until 1914 that American engineer John F. Stevens was able to complete the canal, not by blasting away all the obstacles, but by creating a process for actually *lifting* ships from one level to another, allowing a ship to do the impossible—to travel uphill. The designers of the canal knew something about bringing things "to the next level." The plan looked something like figure 1.

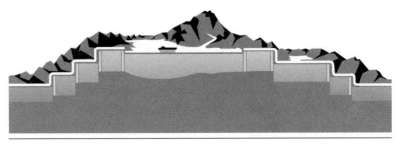

Figure 1.

The ingenious plan provided for the removal of only the highest portion of the mountain and for the building of individual locks designed to raise and lower vessels over the different elevations of the land being crossed. When finished, it looked more like figure 2.

The Panama Parable gives us a picture of the simplicity *and* complexity of moving a youth ministry to that elusive "next level." In each lock of the canal, a ship is raised between twenty-five and thirty feet, not by muscular strength or pure force, but by a complex structure that *simply* applies the natural power of rising and lowering water levels.

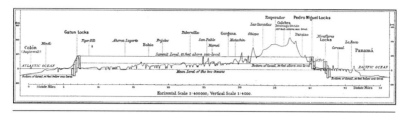

Figure 2.

Typical youth workers employ a far different approach. With passion and commitment to do "whatever it takes," they exert exhausting, often Herculean efforts to move the ministry to the next level. They attempt to heave their boats out of the water and carry them to the next level, instead of creating structures that can access a power greater than their own strength. The heavy lifting of moving their youth ministry from one level to the next too often results in herniated hearts that give up trying altogether.

But there are ways to naturally "raise the water level" in our ministries so that they will move from one level to the other, not by heavy lifting but through the creation of intentional structures. And I am convinced that a vision for such structures is absolutely necessary for churches that want to see lasting change in their youth ministries. Sustainable transformation is not catalyzed by superstars acting independently, however heroically, but by ministry "engineers" who choose to learn how to structure for change.

STRUCTURE FOR CHANGE

How then do we create the series of locks that can move our youth ministries from where they are to where we want them to be? It all starts with that single word *structure.*

Any land animal more than six inches long needs a structure, a skeleton, to survive. And any youth ministry with more than a handful of youth will need one as well. Unfortunately, most youth ministries (and youth ministers) are woefully short on structure.

Most churches frantically try to make it to the next level without building first-level structures. As a result, most churches build house-of-cards youth ministries, programs that expand willy-nilly to the point of implosion.

But sustainable youth ministries do it differently.

SQUARING THE CORNERS: DEVELOPING CONTROL DOCUMENTS

All four walls were up. Our one-room building in the slums of Tijuana was taking shape. Our work had progressed more rapidly than expected. Spirits were high—until our work came to a screeching halt.

Our construction guide asked for a few volunteers to "square the building." As our more agile workers positioned themselves on top of the corners, the rest of us waited for what felt like a very long time.

The grumbling of annoyed youth and leaders ("What's taking so long?" "Come on!") couldn't hurry our site supervisor. He knew what most of the rest of us didn't: taking time to square the house would save exponential amounts of time later.

Sadly, very few churches take the time to "square" their youth ministries. As a result, these ministries waste countless hours re-inventing the wheel each year, compensating for the results of foundational corners that never got squared. In our work with churches, we look for five key documents to confirm that a youth ministry has been "squared":

1. *Directories.* Most churches have lists of their youth, volunteers and visitors, but those lists are usually stored in a variety of arcane computer systems. A sustainable youth ministry starts with a directory of its students (including school, grade, parents' names, phone number and any other information that seems appropriate). The second essential directory is of all volunteers and staff working in the ministry, including each person's contact information and role in the ministry. The final directory includes the names and contact information for all visitors to the youth ministry in the previous two to three years.

There's no hard-and-fast rule for deciding which students belong in the youth directory and which belong in the visitors directory. What's absolutely crucial, though, is that these directories be updated at least annually, using a consistent standard for who does and does not qualify as "ours." As a way of maximizing the accuracy of the directories, we recommend *printing* them annually and distributing them at least to the members of the youth leadership team.

2. *An annual events calendar.* There's no reason for a youth ministry not to have its major-events calendar mapped out at least a year in advance, except laziness. Every September, parents should be able to plan around events, including trips, for the upcoming summer (nine months away). Too many youth ministers complain about the lack of committed volunteers and youth who don't sign up for programs, when those programs are announced less than six weeks before they happen. It's almost impossible to recruit volunteers to take load-bearing responsibility for programs less than six weeks away.

3. *Job descriptions.* When I ask the youth ministers we coach for a copy of their job description, the typical answers are variations on these:

- "I know I've got one, but . . . [nervous laughter]."

- "I haven't looked at it in years."

Everyone from the lead youth staff to the van drivers have a better chance of playing their positions well if we can at least give them, in writing, a document that outlines the scope of their responsibilities. We like to help churches create results-oriented job descriptions, rather than responsibility-oriented ones, an approach that gives latitude to each worker to determine the "how" behind the desired results. (A few sample job descriptions can be found at www.ymarchitects.com.) Note, however, that a job description only gets used to the extent that it is part of a larger process that includes an annual review and revision of it.

4. *The master recruiting list.* Most youth ministries struggle to find volunteers. But very few have a clear process for recruiting the volunteers they need, beyond blanket appeals to overworked church members. A master recruiting list begins the process by first determining exactly how many volunteer leaders are needed for the coming year.

We recommend creating this list in February (when recruiting season opens) and spending a few hours every week calling the most likely prospects, expecting a "no" from two-thirds of them.

Chapter ten describes the priority and process of building a thriving volunteer leadership team. But for now, it will be enough simply to start thinking like a coach. No football coach would ever think of stepping onto the field with only five players. A youth director who runs ahead to start building programs before he or she has a team to run those programs will be perpetually mired in sputtering initiatives that never quite get off the ground. (A sample master recruiting template can be found at www.ymarchitects.com.)

5. *The curriculum template.* We call the final control document a curriculum template, a six- or seven-year game plan of how the teachings in the youth ministry will be structured. There's an almost infinite variety of approaches to developing a curriculum template. The key, though, is to have a plan that's distinct from any specific current curriculum resources. Let me explain.

Most youth ministries have a reactive curriculum "plan," driven primarily by the availability (and marketing) of specific curriculum resources. A curriculum template, on the other hand, provides the framework for a wide variety of resources that might be used. Here are a few examples:

- One church might choose a curriculum template based on the lectionary and match the teachings in the youth ministry to this three-year, crossdenominational plan that ensures exposure to the entire scope of the Bible in three years.

- Another church might buy into the scope and sequence of a denominational curriculum or an independently published resource, such as Student Life.

- Another church might have an annual rotation, ensuring that each year, the youth of the church are exposed to core topics, like Jesus, Old Testament, New Testament, relationships, missions and service, soul-tending, decision-making, and apologetics.

- And still another church might choose to let the flow of the Bible provide the template, beginning each year in Genesis and ending each year in Revelation.

Only after the template is determined should specific curriculum resources be chosen or developed. This approach allows for the certain reality that some curriculum resources won't work and will need to be replaced, *without* having to change the template or the overall plan.

Imagine what would happen if schools taught with the same approach to curriculum that most churches use. One year, a teacher stumbles onto an engaging curriculum on verbs, with some really cool videos on gerunds. When the kids and teachers get bored with that curriculum, they cut it short, and the teacher runs to the curriculum store, finds a compelling study on algebraic equations (narrated by Rob Bell-Curve), and starts to teach that the next week. When that study is winding down, the teacher decides it's time to teach on rocks or medieval knights or Christmas around the world.

There's a good chance that any number of these resources would have commendable components. The failure in the teaching process would not be due to the individual resources but to the lack of a framework to tie those resources together.

Unlike the other control documents (which are straightforward assignments), the development of a clear curriculum template is a complex process that will likely require a much broader buy-in from stakeholders in the youth ministry. (For more information about developing a clear curriculum template, see www.ymarchitects.com.)

The corners are, of course, not the foundation. We build on the foundation of Christ, but before we start building, we've got to make sure we have squared our corners.

PURPOSEFUL STRUCTURE:
DEVELOPING VISIONING DOCUMENTS

Once the control documents are in place, it's time to develop documents that can clarify and provide the roadmap for the future of the youth ministry. We've found that these documents are best developed through a visioning retreat (what we sometimes call the "dance-floor building retreat").

I recently returned from a visioning retreat with one of our client churches, and I was reminded again of why so few churches attend to such things. The debates are too tedious, the rabbit trails too alluring, the axes to grind too anxiety-producing to make such a process anything but exhausting.

When it was over, all that was left in the room was a scattered collection of cups half-full of long-cold coffee, two exhausted youth directors and me. It had taken twenty youth ministry stakeholders and the three of us twelve hours to hammer out a vision for this youth ministry.

Many churches actually have visioning documents for their youth ministries. But more often than not, these statements were written by one person (usually the paid youth worker) in the privacy of his or her office and then slapped on a brochure, only to be ignored for the next few years. Instead of cobbling together a patchwork of good ideas with no strategic thread, a systems approach to creating visioning documents widens the base of support for a youth ministry and galvanizes a team to move together in a single direction.

If a visioning process is to set the course for a youth ministry's future, it will involve a broad group of stakeholders in the ministry, including teachers, youth leaders, elders, youth and parents. But the process of drafting the four visioning documents in a way that propels a ministry forward is no small feat. We use a sometimes tedious and time-consuming process that engages ten to twenty stakeholders (staff, parents, volunteers and sometimes students) over a period of twelve to fifteen hours to craft these four key visioning documents:

1. A mission statement

2. Measurable three-year goals

3. A statement of values

4. An organizational chart

By allowing multiple groups to work on drafting and revising the same documents, we avoid the trap of premature closure, the temptation to accept the first "good enough" idea that the most vocal group member proposes. Without an intentionally crafted process, the development of the visioning documents easily settles into what Patrick Lencioni calls "an atmosphere of self-victimizing groupthink."

Let's look at the nature and purpose of each of the four visioning documents.

1. The youth ministry mission statement. In the midseventies, Harvard University professor Edward Banfield made a profound discovery. He learned that seeing one's life in terms of its long-term trajectory is one of the strongest predictors of a person's future success. More important than education, family background, intelligence or race was the ability to view life from what Banfield called the "long-term perspective."

Those who work with chronically disadvantaged families (those living in poverty for multiple generations) have discovered a curious phenomenon: one item missing from homes of families trapped in generational poverty is a calendar. With little sense of how their actions today will impact how they live in the future, these families find it almost impossible to move from where they are to where they want to be. And consequently, they remain trapped in patterns they never would have chosen.

> Vision—no matter how in line with the vision of Jesus—is never enough. Execution of the vision is what counts. And execution, to a large degree, depends on structure.
>
> ROBERT LEWIS

Too many youth ministries are stuck in the same kind of trap. Driven by the urgent demands of simply keeping a youth ministry afloat, most youth workers define long-range planning as getting this month's calendar done just in time for the newsletter to go out.

But without a clearly articulated, compelling vision of what their church would like for its youth ministry to accomplish, these ministries meander with no higher purpose than simply "having a youth ministry" or "having a youth ministry better than most other churches in town." But this is not a vision; it is a fearful reaction to the risk of extinction.

> Something counterintuitive about growth: You have to do less if you want to grow more. And if you do more, chances are you will grow less.
>
> ANDY STANLEY

A clearly articulated vision protects churches from becoming, in the words of Robert Lewis, "a sort of Christian 'club' that [exhausts] itself trying to keep its members happy." A compelling vision protects youth ministries from competing agendas and paralyzing practices. And a well-crafted mission statement can become the filter through which leaders of a ministry determine which of the hundreds of ideas before them they will actually implement.

We've been fascinated to observe that, in more than a few churches, the first mission statement drafts come back totally devoid of any mention of God, with no mission higher than socializing teenagers into some vague notion of responsible adulthood. Other churches draft a statement that might be more appropriate for a forced labor camp than a youth ministry. But as we continue poking and prodding a bit, the drafting teams go back again (and again) to the drawing board.

When the tired debates about whether youth group should be more fun or more "spiritual" come up, a clear mission statement can help leaders navigate. Of course, many stakeholders would much rather skip the visioning process altogether, preferring to rush into the how-to part of the mission. (Find examples of youth ministry mission statements at www.ymarchitects.com.)

2. Measurable three-year goals. On September 23, 1999, NASA's 125-million-dollar Mars probe ended its ten-month journey prematurely with a crash into the surface of the planet. As the investigation concluded, NASA admitted that the cause of the crash was simple. As I understand it, one engineering team did its calculations with the equivalent of metric units, while another made its calculations using another type of units. The difference was totally unnoticeable early in the journey, but after 416 million miles, the tiny discrepancy widened, until the spacecraft literally *probed* the planet. The method of measurement made all the difference.

Most youth ministers I know are happy not to measure anything. Many bristle at the thought of tracking attendance patterns or setting measurable goals. But without agreed-upon, measurable goals, a youth ministry will suffer from terminal vagueness. A numbers-free youth ministry simply doesn't work for the long haul.

Imagine this conversation:

Youth worker: I'd like to sign our youth group up for a summer mission trip with your organization.

Mission staffer: Great! How many kids would you like to bring?

Youth worker: As many as we can.

Mission staffer: You can bring up to five hundred. How many would you like to bring?

Youth worker: We'll just see how many God brings.

Mission staffer: We can't very well sign your group up unless we know how many you plan to bring. Your deposit will have to be based on that total.

Youth worker: You are *obsessed* with numbers!

Youth workers can be victims of numbers or authors of them. What would happen, I wonder, if youth workers stopped fighting *against* numbers and started taking responsibility for determining what measurements will best help them track the results they want to achieve?

Without clear and measurable goals, the youth ministry is evaluated by as many standards as there are people complaining. Without clear and measurable goals, the only marching order for a youth director is "try to keep as many people happy as possible." Clear, measurable targets can protect youth workers from the pressure to say yes to every new idea that bubbles up from important people in the church, allowing the ministry to defer adding new programs until the time of year when the re-visioning of goals takes place. I've been known to say, "I love that idea, but this year, we are lashed to the mast of these goals that have been established for our youth ministry. But we'd be happy to include your idea when we consider our goals for next year."

As important as the first visioning process is, it's equally important for the youth ministry to have processes in place for evaluating and re-visioning its goals *each and every year*. The youth ministries we work with establish three-year goals, each accompanied by a one-year bench-mark. The three-year goals tend to be "stretch goals," often set twice as high as the ministry hopes to reach, knowing that normal organizations tend to hit 50 percent of their goals. The one-year benchmarks are more attainable, since these are the standards against which the effectiveness of the ministry will be measured annually.

Goals do not necessarily mean that bigger is better. They affirm that clearer is better. Goals help define what a particular ministry will look like as it moves toward increasing health. If we want our youth minis-tries to be evaluated by something *other* than numbers and programs, we must take responsibility to define our targets clearly.

3. A statement of values. Values stand guard over the climate of a youth ministry. The climate or culture of a ministry must never be sac-rificed on the altar of achieving measurable goals. Values protect a youth ministry from becoming so goal-oriented that it sacrifices the things that matter most.

For my wife and me the clearest picture of the powerful, protective role that values play comes from our own home. When our kids were still at home, Susan and I had a *goal*: we wanted them not to live like pigs in our house. Now if, in the process of trying to achieve the goal of having kids with clean rooms, we "motivated" them with anger, bitter-ness and resentment, we would have taught them about a whole lot more than just cleaning their rooms. They would have learned that it's okay to treat people in destructive, disrespectful ways, as long as it helps them achieve the desired results.

Values define the spirit with which we will go about accomplish-ing our goals. For instance, love, kindness and respect are values. One church, which had run off four youth ministers in as many years, named one of their values as "excellence." As we processed together how this value, if left unchecked, could result in a destructive, overactive-white-blood-cell pattern, they chose to add the value of *grace*. Without being intentional about its values, a youth ministry has little power to cultivate a climate of transformation. (Find a few samples of values statements at www.ymarchitects.com.)

4. A structure. There is a (perhaps mythical) story about Napoleon meeting with his counselors before going to war. The counselors, knowing Napoleon's grand visions for expanding his empire, presented their aggressive plan of attack. He listened quietly as each described a different component of their ambitious plan. But with a few short questions from Napoleon, they sulked from the room, commissioned to start over again.

What were Napoleon's questions? He simply asked about horses. "How many do we have? Where will they all be placed?" In a few short minutes, the humiliated counselors realized that their plans, though ambitious, would quickly *outrun the available horses*.

Ambitious churches often design grand schemes for success that simply outrun their available horses. I've spoken with more than a few senior pastors who express their hope for a youth ministry that will engage four hundred to five hundred youth a week. But few seem to have any idea of how many resources it will take to sustain such a ministry. And so the church hires a youth staff woefully inadequate for accomplishing the church's ambitious vision—a recipe for nonsustainability.

Getting a handle on how many horses a strategic plan will require demands a clear definition of the organization's structure.

> Without an Organization Chart, everything hinges on luck and good feelings, on the personalities of the people and the goodwill they share. Unfortunately, personalities, good feelings, goodwill and luck aren't the only ingredients of a successful organization; alone, they are the recipe for chaos and disaster.
>
> MICHAEL GERBER

All organizations are hierarchical. At each level people serve under those above them. An organization is therefore a structured institution. If it is not structured, it is a mob. Mobs do not get things done. They destroy things.

THEODORE LEVITT

In almost every visioning retreat I've done, someone resists the idea of a traditional organizational chart, recommending instead something more organic, maybe a three-dimensional matrix chart or one with less layers, more like a series of concentric circles than a hierarchy. My experience has been that, though I appreciate the creativity and outside-the-box thinking that these folks bring to the table, attempts at creativity with an organizational chart typically result in fuzzy definitions of who is responsible for what, the very opposite of the purpose of such a chart. (For a few samples of youth ministry organizational charts, go to www.ymarchitects.com.)

RE-VISIONING: WHEN IT'S TIME FOR CHANGE

Though visioning is a powerful process for churches struggling to get their youth ministries on solid footing, it would be a mistake to see it as a one-time event. The ideal timing may differ for different ministries, but we recommend an annual review of these documents, with a focus on revising the organizational chart and job descriptions, and re-upping the three-year goals and the one-year benchmarks. After the visioning documents are set the first time and the trajectory of the ministry is in place, the annual revisiting can be completed in much less time than the first time around.

But every five years or so, we also recommend that key stakeholders gather again for a more thorough vision-casting time (not unlike the first visioning experience). For example, one church might spend five years on stabilizing its youth ministry and building an appropriate infrastructure. But at the end of that time, with a ministry appropriately funded and staffed, with a strong team of volunteers and a new tradition of effective long-range planning in place, the ministry would be ready to set a new vision that can capture and reengage the hearts of those investing in the youth ministry.

Unfortunately, instead of revisioning after five years of stability, most ministries simply choose to coast. But, as in sailing, the time to tack is when you have enough momentum to make the turn. If you wait too long, the boat will stall and leave you dead in the water. The time to change the strategic direction of your ministry is, ironically, when things are going well.

Every organization goes through predictable cycles. As a new initiative begins or a new staff person is hired, increased momentum comes as a natural consequence. When momentum is strong and energy is high, the last thing most churches are thinking about is changing something. But the best time to consider a new initiative or a new trajectory in youth ministry is just before the momentum of the current focus has peaked. We picture it like this:

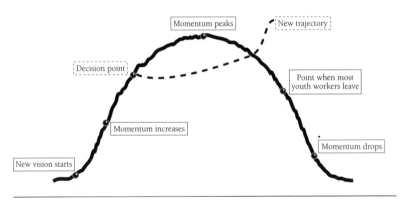

Figure 3.

In the evolution of a typical youth ministry, a new hire often initiates a "new era." Curiosity combines with the infusion of new ideas and a new personality to give a natural lift to the ministry. After a few years, the patterns and programs of the not-so-new staff person are well established, and parts of the ministry are beginning to fly on autopilot. There's a general sense of contentment about the youth ministry, and though not perfect, the paid youth worker is appreci-

Many times we lose our momentum because we are afraid to lose the success we've achieved, and before we know it, we discover that we are running on empty.

ERWIN McMANUS

ated by most stakeholders in the ministry. It's at this season, when contentment is at its highest, that the youth ministry may be in the most danger.

If, instead of coasting in contentment, the youth ministry reengages in bold dreaming and engaging innovation, the seeds of fresh, new life can be planted in the ministry. Apart from this kind of innovative thinking, the youth pastor will grow increasingly frustrated and will eventually leave just about the time the decline of the program has begun to reach top speed.

In their classic book *In Search of Excellence,* Tom Peters and Robert Waterman found that one of the most dangerous things that can happen to a company is for it to become large and successful, because its leaders so easily forget "what got them big in the first place: *innovation.*" The National Science Foundation discovered that "small firms produced about four times as many innovations per research-and-development dollar as medium-sized firms, and about twenty-four times as many as large firms."

BUILDING DIFFERENTLY

I remember my first foray into building model airplanes. I brought home the box with the cool picture on it, only to be disappointed by the gazillion gray plastic pieces inside, looking much more tedious than I had expected. I went to the directions—"Glue Wing Staff T-3 to Elbow Cog M"—and dutifully followed the instructions. But within a few minutes I was frustrated, bored.

I wanted to get on with the good stuff—building the wings or the fuselage, putting on the decals. So, laying aside the instructions, I went ahead and glued the big pieces together. Now I was making progress! Or so I thought.

As I returned to the instructions, I realized that I'd need to unglue the big pieces to put all the small pieces where they belonged. My solution? Leave the model kit in pieces, watch cartoons and eat another peanut butter Nutter Butter Sandwich Cookie. After a month of walking around the pile of pieces, I decided I must not be cut out for building models.

As a matter of habit, youth workers of sustainable ministries do those tedious, little things that "normal" (that is, frustrated, stagnant, victim-oriented) youth workers find inconvenient (like recruiting volunteers, calling fringe kids and learning something new every day). Long-term, effective youth workers do different things with their time. Oh, they still return phone calls; they still attend meetings; they still meet with students. But they do them in a different order.

NOW WHAT?

If you're reading this chapter as a professional youth worker, I think I can guess what's going through your mind right about now: "I have trouble enough just keeping the ministry running. How in the world am I going to develop all these visioning documents, much less track our progress on a regular basis? I'm sure it's a great idea, but I just don't have time."

Am I close?

As youth workers ourselves, those of us on the Youth Ministry Architects team have recognized that the most important stuff, the long-term strategic stuff, seldom happens naturally. In fact, one of the main reasons our ministry exists is because we recognize that, while most youth workers do fine with the week-to-week programming, almost all of us struggle to keep our eye on the long-term priorities as well. But whether you choose to initiate the crafting of these documents for yourself or you invite someone to oversee the process for you, you'll want to make a priority of clarifying your ministry's vision with the clear architectural documents outlined in this chapter.

6

CHANGING CULTURE

The Work of the Environmental Architect

e·thos—noun—1. the fundamental character or spirit of a culture; the underlying sentiment that informs the beliefs, customs, or practices of a group or society; dominant assumptions of a people or period. 2. the character or disposition of a community, group, person, etc.
DICTIONARY.COM

Failure and success are not episodes, they are trajectories.
ROSABETH MOSS KANTER

Nothing good happens by accident.
PETER DRUCKER

Almost every longing related to youth ministry is connected to a single desire: We want to *change something*.

Sometimes that desire is simple and straightforward: "I want to get my youth committee out from under the children's committee on the organizational chart." Others are more far-reaching and global: "I want to move my youth from apathy toward becoming more fully devoted followers of Christ." And still others are plainly pragmatic: "How can we get more kids involved?" or "How can I recruit more leaders?"

But beneath them all is the same fundamental passion: the drive to create change.

Those who learn to be change agents impact almost everything they touch. And those who never learn this skill stay trapped on a treadmill of frustration, working with greater and greater intensity but traveling nowhere. These treadmill captives are often the quickest to fall victim to the attitudes of youth ministry's doomsday prophets who declare, "Youth ministry just doesn't work anymore."

We've discovered that just the opposite is true. Youth ministry *does*, in fact, "work," and it does so with almost predictable regularity. In a wide variety of contexts, across a wide variety of denominations, there *are* youth ministries that have learned to catalyze change, not only in young people's lives but in their churches as well. More often than not, when we find those youth ministries, we also discover that a particular kind of culture has been established, a culture in which leaders don't simply *push* for change, they *cultivate* it.

In the last chapter, we looked at the core *structures* that initiate and sustain strategic change—the *architecture* of transformation. But beyond and beneath the work of the architect (with the blueprints, the steps, the strategies and structures), there are deeper, more fundamental processes that impact change, what we call the work of the alchemist.

Alchemists (and the chemists who later followed in their footsteps) did not simply engage in processes in which 1 + 1 simply equals 2. Rather, by combining chemical compounds, the alchemist combined substances, which, in an almost magical way, formed an entirely different substance altogether. 1 + 1 equals 12.

Any attempt to architect the "hard" structures of a youth ministry (e.g., control documents, visioning documents, recruitment processes, etc.) will produce little lasting change if those efforts are not combined with at least equal attention to the "soft" attitudes—culture and values (the atmosphere)—that lie beneath those structures. Though sociologists refer to this social atmosphere as the ethos or culture of a group, throughout this chapter I'll be using the term *climate,* because terms like "ice cold" or "warmed up" or "stormy" give us not just the meaning of the terms but their *feel* as well.

CLIMATE CONTROL

Most new youth workers step into their roles with the luxury of inexperience, armed with little more than raw enthusiasm to love kids and lead them to Jesus. Certainly not a bad start. But because so few come with any awareness or training in the power of climate in ministry, many are set up for failure from the start. They may know how to find skits and programs and curriculums and websites; they might even know how to do contact work and network with other youth workers. But they all must, if they are to navigate the turbulent waters of ministry, do something much more foundational.

I like to call it environmental architecture (a term borrowed from Erwin McManus). An environmental architect begins with the confession that we have no power to *make* young people grow. We cannot make our churches or youth ministries or senior pastors into what we want them to be. We cannot make parents, volunteers and students do what we want them to do. What we can do is create an environment in which this kind of growth and change is not only possible, but probable.

Think greenhouse. A greenhouse is a place where living things grow well, a place protected from the unpredictability of the elements, where fragile plants are able to grow strong regardless of the conditions outside. Fragile plants thrive when the climate is controlled. The right temperature, light, food and water supply produce living things that grow strong enough to thrive in a more hostile environment. In the same way, the environmental architect focuses on creating climate in his or her youth ministry, spending very little time worrying about the climate outside, those things that can't be controlled, like busy kids, complaining parents, demanding senior pastors.

Periodically I get calls from people who ask if they can come to observe our youth ministry. I warn them to prepare to be underwhelmed. By the time they leave, I can see it on their faces. They don't say it, but I know what they're thinking: "We could do *that!* Why is it working here but not for us back home, when our programs are actually *better* than these?"

As much as I might hate to admit it, they're usually right. It's not that we *try* to have mediocre programs; it's just that they seem to happen with disappointing regularity. Yet the ministry continues to thrive. We continue to see surprising transformation in young people's lives. After two decades of doing ministry in the same setting, I've begun to discover why.

Transformation doesn't happen primarily because specific tasks get accomplished or because of consistently excellent programs. Transformation becomes habitual for a youth ministry when a unique "climate of transformation" is established. I'm afraid I had to learn that lesson the hard way.

THE HIGH COST OF IGNORING CLIMATE

A few years back, I helped to lead the charge at our traditional church to move us toward an alternative, "less traditional" option for worship. We *structured* the process almost perfectly. We established a subcommittee of the worship committee, and they did their work well. They presented a strong case to our elders. And the elders, though a bit uneasy about the unsettledness such a move might create in the congregation, affirmed the report of the Alternative Worship Subcommittee and gave the green light to move forward.

So we went to work, diligently planning our first month of alternative services. We established prayer groups, wrote promotional newsletter articles, made plans to ensure that the gymnasium would be full on those Sunday mornings.

But we never thought about the climate.

The seven-week experiment came and went. We assumed that the overwhelming support of hundreds of people in the congregation would be enough to sustain approval. What we ignored was that the "success" of our very structured process had sharply divided the congregation. Within a month or so, that fissure erupted into a bitter battle from which it took us years to recover.

We had a game plan fully in place. The rationale for the change was airtight. We had attended to creating the vision; we were willing to do the work. But a vision statement and a strategic plan were not enough. Because our programmatic changes totally ignored the importance of creating the right culture, the well-intentioned plans withered like tomato plants in the Sahara.

If instead we had paid attention to climate first, if we had been careful to listen to the concerns of those who were "opposed" to the innovation, if we had paused and paced the implementation process, things might have ended very differently. Instead, we naively assumed that the "approval" of our elders gave us license to ignore the climate of distrust surrounding the content issue. We were wrong.

CLIMATE, VISION, TASKS

Ask any youth director what his or her job is and chances are you'll hear a list of tasks: "I hang out with kids," "I teach the Bible," "I go to meetings." Sadly, most youth workers are almost obsessively focused on tasks. They react to the demands placed before them, daily racing against the clock to try to get more done in less time, to get all the phone calls and emails answered, all the lessons written, the programs prepared. But eventually, almost every youth worker, no matter how organized, realizes that there is simply not enough time to get all the tasks completed.

The completion of a fragmented set of tasks, as much diligence as that process might require, can be the very thing that prevents youth workers from building momentum for their ministries. When this realization comes, it's not unusual for a youth worker (or a church) to send out the call for a "vision."

And the scurry of meetings begins. We've seen churches spend hundreds of volunteer and staff hours to hammer out a vision for the youth ministry, write mission statements and values statements, prepare measurable goals. The best of these create structures that keep the visioning documents consistently before those responsible for building the ministry. But sadly, vision, in itself, is not enough.

Too often, even the most compelling vision is thwarted because, in spite of all the right structures being in place, little to no attention has been given to the climate. Like working in a building that's structurally sound but filled with noxious gases, these youth ministries may have a fine, well-structured vision. But the climate is toxic, preventing sustainable change from ever taking hold.

THE USUAL YOUTH MINISTRY PYRAMID

Here's the way we picture the approach of most youth ministries, starting with tasks, moving to vision and seldom (if ever) finding time to create the right kind of climate:

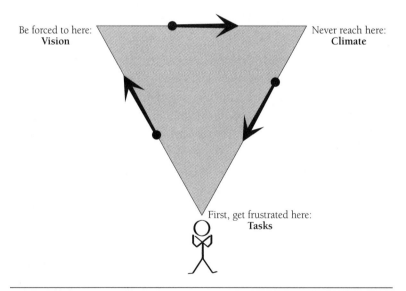

Figure 4.

This process is exactly the opposite of a ministry that becomes sustainable. You'll notice that the pyramid here is upside down, with all the weight of responsibility placed on the shoulders of a single person. The person at the bottom of the pyramid—typically the youth director—gets less and less done, and the work that does get done seems more like a chore than a calling.

At this point, it's normal for a youth worker to fall into a victim mindset and begin complaining about the unrealistic expectations and lack of support from the church, the parents, the students. With frustration bubbling over, the youth worker is asked (sometimes demanded) to create a vision for the youth ministry.

But the visioning that occurs at this point typically takes place in a very tense climate, both for the youth worker, who knows the process has been created because people are criticizing his or her work, and for the parents, whose dissatisfaction with the youth ministry has become acute. And so the anxiety-driven vision simply raises the expectations of those who are already frustrated, often compounding the negativity.

Of course, the climate of negativity continues to poison the youth director, who becomes even more obsessively focused on the completion of tasks. But now, he or she is expected to complete all the additional tasks required by the new vision.

Too often the acrimonious and divisive departure of the failing youth director sends the church even further into the negative. The "vision" is put in a file drawer somewhere, awaiting the arrival of a new youth director, who will step into the same toxic climate and likely be overwhelmed by the same tasks that plagued the previous youth worker. And the cycle starts all over again.

FLIPPING THE PYRAMID

But what would happen if we flipped the pyramid?

A systems approach to youth ministry places the first focus on climate, not tasks. In the context of a healthy climate, a vision is developed. Only then can a church hope for its youth ministry to manage its tasks and content issues well.

If church leaders express one desire more consistently than any other, it's their wish for more kids to be involved in the life of the church.

These are not numbers-obsessed tyrants. They're typically godly men and women who simply want to see the church be more faithful not only in nurturing its own children in the faith but also in engaging the kids who stand outside the normal reach of the church.

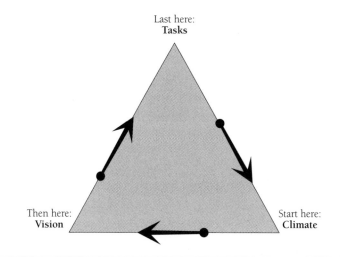

Figure 5.

Our experience has been consistent: we've never seen a youth ministry with a *singular* focus on boosting numbers actually be successful. More often than not, an urgent demand for numbers has just the opposite effect: increasing the level of toxic anxiousness in the climate surrounding the youth ministry, resulting in *less,* not more, youth becoming involved.

Sometimes the shortest distance between two points is *not* a straight line, and sometimes an obsessive focus on getting results as quickly as possible is the slowest path to achieving sustainable results. (Again, we need look no further than the initial attempts to build the Panama Canal.)

Several years ago, we began working with a committed, enthusiastic, gifted youth worker in a wealthy church that had struggled for years with getting its youth ministry off the ground. The youth director undoubtedly had the right combination of gifts—a deep love for Christ, an engaging, fiery personality, and a commitment to do whatever it would take to create a thriving, sustainable ministry. Quite honestly, I assumed transformation would come quickly, easily within a year.

So we set to work building a sustainable foundation for this ministry, deliberately attending to structure and climate. But within the first six months of the building process, we discovered termites: a highly anxious colleague who undermined the youth director's every attempt to build the youth ministry, multiple agendas whispered by volunteers who had little interest in being connected to the church, and a volunteer in his midtwenties surreptitiously dating one of the girls in the high-school group. All these combined to hamstring any effort to structure an effective youth ministry.

Now, after three long years of tenaciously attending to the systemic climate issues, the youth ministry has righted itself and *begun* to grow. It is often in the process of "failing forward" that youth workers learn to manage the culture of their ministries, rather than becoming victims of their ministry's culture.

A PRIMER ON ENVIRONMENTAL ARCHITECTURE

So, if we are to achieve a different starting point for our ministries, if we are to be environmental architects who work to create the right climate for our youth ministries, where do we begin? We've discovered the five decisions that most profoundly affect the building of a healthy climate: delivering results, trusting the process, importing joy into the chaos, embracing stories and metaphors, and instilling rituals and traditions.

1. *We deliver results.* By far the most dramatic way to change the climate of a youth ministry is to provide its stakeholders with visible evidence that something good actually is happening. Nothing accelerates climate change quite like speeding up the results.

To illustrate, I don't have to look any farther than across town at the Vanderbilt Commodore football program. A few years ago, the team was in the middle of its predictable losing season. No one expected much more than one or two games where Vandy would spoil the hopes of some SEC football powerhouse. Few even held out hope for a winning season. But all that changed the day after a visit to Neyland Stadium in Knoxville, a game in which the Commodores broke their twenty-plus-year losing streak to the University of Tennessee. If you happened to be in Nashville the week after that game, you would have thought our 'Dores had just won the Super Bowl. One key win *dramatically* shifted the climate.

To begin tilting the climate of a youth ministry in a positive direction, its leaders need to identify a small victory, a single visible result, and go after it. The climate of a youth ministry can change with something as simple as recruiting a new team of volunteers (and commissioning them in front of the church). Another church tipped its youth ministry toward a healthy climate with a single mission trip that attracted just a handful more students than the year before.

> Churches are a lot like horses—they don't like to be startled or surprised. It causes wild behavior. . . . If you're the lead youth worker, fast changes can appear arrogant or reveal a maverick's personality to your church.
>
> DOUG FIELDS

A small victory can begin the process of climate change. But sustaining such a change requires a pattern of little victories tied together by the climate-control processes that follow.

2. We trust the process. Moving from where we are to where we want to be takes time—so much time, in fact, that many youth directors short-circuit the process. If we're going to engineer a climate of transformation for our youth ministries, we will not do it by stepping in with guns blazing.

Sustainable change happens when leaders recognize the power of incremental revolution, the power of one small change after another, until the incremental changes result in exponential change. Architecting a healthy climate for ministry is usually a lot more like growing bamboo than like a construction project.

Try watching bamboo grow sometime. (You won't be entertained.) After waiting for weeks, then months, then up to three years, you may begin to wonder whether your plant has issues. You might compare your inferior specimen to the other successful bamboo plants you've seen. You might be tempted to exhume your mutant plant, to analyze its problems.

But people who know bamboo relax when they see no visible signs of growth in the first few years. They know the process, and they trust it. If the environmental conditions are right, eventually the tipping point comes, and growth happens. In fact, some bamboo plants, when they hit their growth season, can grow up to four feet in twenty-four hours.

Those of us who work with junior-high-schoolers know the feeling, don't we? For years we wonder if we'll ever see signs of change, if anything is sinking in. Then suddenly the process takes hold, and those young people begin to explode with questions, with honesty, often with compassion and faithfulness that must have been buried beneath the surface for years.

Too many churches and youth ministers distrust the process and find themselves changing focus every few years, gambling their hopes on the next superstar on the court. As a result, they never experience the profound momentum that builds when a team moves together in the same direction for years.

3. We import joy into the chaos. Once every few months, I meet with Andy, my spiritual director. For the past six years, he has prodded me, listened to me and pointed me to a life truly lived "in Christ." In the first year of our visits together, Andy noticed that I'd almost always come to his office rushed, apologetic for being late, embarrassed that I had so little control over my life. More than once, he looked at me and said something like this: "Creative chaos . . . it's the way you were made. It's where you thrive. Stop fighting it." Furrowing the eyebrows, tightening the muscles and working harder is seldom the answer. In fact, seriousness, anxiousness and drivenness can work against us, sabotaging our efforts at making progress.

In his book *Emotional Intelligence,* Daniel Goleman tells of a study that revealed the power of a joyful climate in maximizing people's ability to solve problems. In this study, two groups were given the very same problem and asked to solve it. The only difference between the groups was that the first watched a video of funny television bloopers before trying to solve the puzzle. The second went straight to work. The laughing groups were consistently better at solving the puzzles (another word for "problems") than the folks who went straight to work.

Family-systems experts suggest that the only way to impact a stuck system is to maintain a non-anxious presence in it, to do more than just react. Many youth workers find themselves in a highly reactive posture, blaming their senior pastors or critical parents for "making them mad." But youth workers who successfully initiate change in their churches have learned to maintain a playful detachment from those triggers that cause people to spiral into negativity and reactive blaming.

4. We instill stories and metaphors. The Hopi proverb is right: "The one who tells the stories rules the world." If we want to create a climate of transformation, we'll do so by creating an "intentional mythology" for our ministries.

Consider the positive mythology created around a building project. There's the thrill of visiting the site, seeing the progress from week to week, walking people through the skeleton frame, imagining what each room will be used for. Though there's a mess everywhere, though the space is totally unusable, excitement still grows because *the mess is seen as a part of the process.*

> **The primary skill for leaders is the ability to clarify and reconceptualize stories, essentially to be one of the best storytellers around the campfire.**
>
> DIANA BUTLER BASS

Youth ministries in a building or remodeling phase are often more of a mess than a construction site. But without someone to tell the story of what's coming, without someone to re-mythologize the mess, complaints and criticism can become overwhelming.

Every youth ministry is either buoyed up or dragged down by its mythology, by the stories and metaphors used to describe it. For most youth ministries, this mythology is almost entirely accidental. But those of us who lead have the power (and responsibility) to craft the stories that will define the climate of our ministries.

Almost every struggling youth ministry we've worked with has been surrounded by a mythology of negativity, a mythology that almost guarantees that the ministry will remain stuck. Consider the impact these kinds of stories and metaphors (all of which we've overheard) might have on a youth ministry:

- "It's on a downward spiral. I don't know what it will take to pull it back up, but it doesn't seem like anything is working."

- "Our youth group is like a patchwork quilt made by somebody who's color blind."

- "We're floundering."

- "The youth group is no longer attractive. That's been lost."

- "We've hit bottom."

- "Over the past few years, attendance has declined tremendously."

- "There seems to be a gap in our church when it comes to youth. When you get to sixth through twelfth grades, there's no curriculum and not enough teachers."

- "It's hard to stand by and watch things crash and burn without things being addressed. No one is doing anything."

- "It's like Death Eaters have come and sucked the life out of our youth group."

As we listened to comments like these from youth and adults in churches around the country, we couldn't help but wonder if the struggles of these youth ministries were not compounded and reinforced by a mythology of hopelessness.

In *The Friendship Factor,* Alan McGinnis describes an experiment in a second-grade classroom. Psychologists observed a teacher who told the children in her class to sit down an average of seven times every twenty minutes (obviously with limited success). When the teacher increased her demands that students sit down to 27.5 times in twenty minutes, misbehavior *increased* significantly.

At the prompting of the psychologists, the teacher tried something different. Instead of telling the "problem" children to sit down, she affirmed and encouraged the students who *were* sitting down. The result? Behavior improved dramatically.

Children—and churches—tend to live into the words that are spoken about them. Focusing on the negative gets more negative, while focusing on the positive results in a much more positive climate.

Leaders of thriving youth ministries are harbingers of what God is doing and is about to do. They're the bards of their youth ministries, telling students and leaders the tales of who they are and what God is up to. They're the environmental experts, cultivating the ethos by seeding it with stories and metaphors that affirm that, although the picture is not yet completed, signs of progress are popping up all around.

5. We embrace rituals and traditions, signs and symbols. Allentown Presbyterian Church is a strange place. With about five hundred people in worship on an average Sunday, this small-town church in New Jersey often has more than two hundred youth each week attending its youth groups. Led mostly by parents who never got the memo that kids didn't want them around, this extraordinary ministry has the kind of climate most youth ministries long for.

The first time I visited, I was struck by the power of its rituals and traditions, little things like lighted candles on the tables (even in the presence of junior-high boys) and the way the tables and chairs were magically taken down by kids after dinner. But one tradition gave me (and anyone who walked through the door) a powerful picture of who this group is: every person who entered the room was greeted in the same way—with cheers and applause. Is it any wonder the biggest problem facing this ministry is what to do with all the kids who keep coming?

Each year on the first weekend of May, our youth ministry sponsors an event we affectionately call Crud Day. To the outside observer, it's nothing more than a typical messy youth group event. But for us, it's one of our most important rites of passage. You see, Crud Day takes place on the afternoon of Confirmation Sunday, when the sixth-graders who've just completed the confirmation process make their profession of faith before the entire church. As these youth move from childhood into the youth group, we mark their transition by putting them on teams with youth from all the other grades. The mud, shaving cream and water balloons give a clear message: "You are one of us. You belong."

When I was a teenager, seemingly insignificant traditions and rituals held our small youth group together. Whether it was the fact that we all spoke with equally unrecognizable accents when we were together or the nickname we used for the senior pastor, our identity was confirmed. Those very traditions and rituals had the power to create and sustain a climate that fed personal transformation for many of us, despite the fact that the content of our programs left something to be desired.

Closely related to rituals and traditions are signs and symbols. Signs and symbols have a way of locking in a group's rituals and traditions. Some groups create a logo; others invite youth to paint their names, their handprints or their favorite Scriptures on the wall of the youth room; still other churches collect pictures for years and present a photo album of memories to students when they graduate.

When we dropped our youngest daughter off at college this year, I couldn't help but notice the signs and symbols she placed around her room—posters of music groups, pictures of friends *and* the silver communion cup she was given at our church's senior banquet as a reminder not only of her identity in Christ but also of her connection to her church family.

Whether the symbol is something as simple as a pneumonic rock (a single "reminder" stone given to students at the end of a class or youth group) or a baby pin presented at the end of a class, signs and symbols help establish a climate in which community identity can be cultivated.

Changing the climate of our churches is hard, but often not as hard as changing ourselves. In the coming chapters, you'll find a few practices that we've found to be the greatest accelerators for change in the youth ministries and youth workers we've had the privilege of working with, practices that we hope can provide baby steps for transforming the climate and structure of your ministry.

7

SEARCHING RIGHT

A Primer for Youth Ministry Search Teams

We encouraged volunteers to think of themselves not as people who run errands to keep a program going but as spiritual directors in the lives of students.

CHRIS FOLMSBEE

You may think that the successful implementation of a management strategy is dependent on finding amazingly competent managers— people with finely honed "people skills," with degrees from management schools, with highly sophisticated techniques for dealing with and developing their people.

It isn't.

You don't need such people.

Nor can you afford them.

In fact, they will be the bane of your existence.

What you need, instead, is a management strategy.

MICHAEL GERBER

The Church of the Good Shepherd had seen five disappointing youth directors appear and disappear in three short years. When this church contacted us, they seemed to be suffering from a chronic case of search committee amnesia, having convinced themselves that, in spite of their consistent 0-5 record, they were simply suffering from a string of bad luck.

Amazingly, when we arrived, the church leaders were energized, not because their youth ministry was moving forward but because they had "successfully" removed their previous youth director. I could just imagine their search team meetings—huddling together around a conference table, thinking positive thoughts and repeating the mantra, "This time we'll find the right one."

We explained that blind optimism could not be a long-term solution, that they would never find the "right" staff person until they had become the right kind of church (or at least the right kind

> One day someone else will be doing what you are doing. Whether you have an exit strategy or not, ultimately, you will exit.
>
> ANDY STANLEY

of youth ministry). When the right kind of system is in place, we suggested, a moderately gifted staff person would thrive.

So we began asking the hard questions: What might there be about the way the Church of the Good Shepherd has been doing youth ministry that would cause its youth staff to spiral into failure with such consistent regularity? And might there be something about the climate of the congregation that had become so toxic that it turned capable youth workers into "the wrong kind of people" for the job?

After the information gathering was complete, our first recommendation was the last thing this group wanted to hear. We suggested that the church postpone its search for replacement staff for a few months until they had built their foundational infrastructure—in other words, that they not hire the dancer until the dance floor had been repaired.

As we entered into the dance-floor restoration process, helping the church hire interim staff, the predictable soon began to happen: anxious church members had all kinds of Easy Buttons to recommend—purposes, programs, promotion plans. In short, almost everyone wanted a new dance to begin—and begin immediately. But the leaders in the youth ministry—the 0-5 team—knew that following this tried and true method would likely result in the same mangled mess the previous youth workers had experienced.

> The view that youth ministry is a place where pastoral leaders "do time" until they qualify for "real" ministry is alive and well, thanks to the self-defeating practice of throwing clergy, seminarians, and unsuspecting volunteers with little experience and less support into positions where adolescents, searching for fidelity, demand more than we have to give.
>
> KENDA DEAN

WOULD THE REAL INTERIM PLEASE STAND UP?

In my twenty-plus years as the youth pastor at First Presbyterian Church in Nashville, I've seen more than my fair share of transitions. Of my eight bosses (count 'em, eight), five of them have had the title "interim." By the time the third or fourth interim rolled around, I came to a profound realization: *everyone* is an interim.

We all have to make our exit someday. It's true for every human being, with most of us getting to serve on the earth less than a single century. It's true in business, where few great CEOs last longer than an "interim" of twenty years. It's particularly true in ministry, acutely so in youth ministry.

The average youth minister serves a single church for 3.9 years. And even those of us who blow the curve with a longer tenure are, just the same, interims.

Think about the role of interims: they proactively prepare the way for a future *that does not include them*. Interims are midwives, not mothers. Interims help a congregation recognize, celebrate and stand guard over its core, momentum-building traditions.

Good youth ministers know that to build their ministries around themselves and *their* relationships with students is to fail in their calling. Though a church's ministry may thrive in the short-run under an interim-centered approach, the long-term result will be less than positive. Like a hub being pulled out of the center of a wheel, each time a staff person pulls out, momentum stalls. Whether the church is left grieving or grateful, each successive leader leaves the church no further along in the journey, with the unspoken expectation that the next "interim" will have to start back at square one.

What would happen if we didn't change our youth ministry model or vision or structure each time there was a staff change? What if we designed our ministries with the very real probability that our youth staff may be around less than four years? What would happen if every youth director (every minister, for that matter) placed the word *interim* in front of his or her title?

Those of us in ministry might free ourselves just a bit from the tantalizing illusion of our own indispensability. Maybe that interim title would help churches and search committees come to grips with the fact that they are never searching for *the* youth director but for someone who can, for a season, steward a vision much larger than themselves.

SEARCH COMMITTEES AND THE ILLUSION OF "PERMANENT" STAFF

I never cease to be amazed that churches are surprised when they have to search again for a new youth staff person. They say things like, "We just weren't expecting this." From my vantage point, it's like saying, "Christmas just snuck up on me this year," or "This bill for my car insurance came out of nowhere."

Okay, maybe it's not as predictable as the annual holiday season, but every church large enough to hire youth staff needs to have a plan in place, not just for hiring the next person, but also for hiring those who will follow. But almost none do. When is the last time you heard of a youth ministry with a succession plan, a plan for how the church will transition seamlessly from one youth staff person to another?

It's time for us to stop obsessing over the "problem" of short-term youth directors and simply build on the landscape we've been given: by and large, most churches will be utilizing short-term youth workers whether they choose to or not. Most churches simply can't afford the alternative.

When an anxious, crisis-oriented church searches for a professional youth worker to solve all its problems, that church faces only two possibilities:

1. The new youth worker is everything the church has prayed for and dreamed of (I've actually never seen this happen, but I suppose it is theoretically possible), or

2. He or she isn't.

If the church has hired someone in the second category (which is almost always the case), the church will face only three not-so-pleasant options:

1. Wallow in an ineffective program until that person chooses to resign.

2. Ask that person to resign, knowing that, more than likely, his or her departure will happen under a cloud of controversy that has the potential to polarize the youth ministry, if not the entire church.

3. Wait five years for the person to grow into being effective in his or her role (typically about the time a youth worker considers moving on).

But what if the church's gamble pays off? What if they're fortunate enough to hire "just the right person"?

The results can actually be worse.

The new youth director likely will create a spike in enthusiasm for the program as their new vision for youth ministry is implemented. At this point, the church will face just two possibilities:

1. The church will enjoy the benefits of being one of the tiny number of churches whose youth director stays ten years or more, or

2. It won't.

A church that heads down this staff-centered track may naturally experience a transition not unlike the Alabama football team after the departure of Bear Bryant in 1982. Since that time, the past-powerhouse bounced from one floundering season to the next, from one hoped-for superstar coach to the next and the next and the next.

We've seen a discouragingly similar pattern in churches with once-thriving youth ministries: churches whose youth programs flounder through three or four post-glory-days youth directors, until finally someone picks their head up and recognizes that their superstar left them with little more than a house of cards, just waiting to fall when he or she pulled out. Each successive "permanent" youth director builds on little more than the ashes of the golden years, with a ministry no further along than before the original superstar first arrived.

THE BETTER WAY

We get more calls and emails from churches searching for youth staff than for any other reason. The callers are laser focused on a single question: Can you help us with our search?

But after much soul searching (and a few mistakes along the way), we made the firm decision that we would never *just* help a church search for its next youth director. We determined to help churches with their searches, but only when it's *a part* of helping those churches get their systems (their architecture and atmosphere) right.

Though this policy has frustrated many would-be clients, the words of Doug Fields kept ringing in our ears: "I've heard too many horror stories of men and women who've been emotionally abused, fired, hurt, or who have left youth ministry because their blind enthusiasm matched a church's desperation for a youth worker and everyone said yes before knowing enough about one another."

To provide search services for a church that has not first built an infrastructure that will allow its staff to thrive would simply perpetuate the illusion that all a youth ministry really needs is "the right person."

When we recommend a systems approach to staffing a youth ministry, some assume that we're suggesting that making the right hire doesn't matter. Nothing could be further from the truth. Ironically, we agree with Tom Paterson's simple mantra, "Get the right person in the right job and the problems will melt away." But the system must be in place first.

THREE ESSENTIAL STAFF ROLES

On any successful building site, there are three essential jobs, and the more complex the building, the more important it is to separate these roles. In the youth ministries we've observed, the same three positions are essential. Though there are rare instances when all three are present in one person, we've not seen it often.

1. *The craftsperson.* This is someone who can do the hands-on building. Though laborers and craftspeople come with various skill sets, their primary focus is not on designing but on following a designer's plans. This is not someone who will be thinking about the big picture but who will do excellent work completing assigned projects—electrical, woodworking, plumbing and so on.

The craftsperson has very clear direction about what he or she is to do. But in the absence of a general contractor, the craftsperson can easily lose focus and be diverted into redesigning the whole building.

In youth ministry, the craftsperson is typically an inexperienced, enthusiastic young adult who has the ability to build relationships with students, develop creative programming and sleep (or not) comfortably on gym floors. It's not unusual for a church to hire a craftsperson and expect him or her to oversee the larger issues of the ministry as well. Such a decision may be the most common structural reason that youth ministries never get off the ground.

2. *The general contractor.* This is someone who can supervise the work and make sure that all the right steps are being completed according to the design. The general contractor is usually the first one to work and the last one to leave, making sure the materials are on site when needed and that laborers with the right skills are present. The general contractor hires or recruits workers and coordinates everyone's work so that the various laborers don't work against each other, such as finishing the drywall before the wiring is in.

Like the craftsperson, the general contractor doesn't *create* the plans for the building. He or she simply "works the plan" designed by architects and engineers, who are trained to design buildings that don't fall down. It's normal, therefore, for the general contractor to spend a good bit of time in conversation with the "architect in the trailer" (below) for troubleshooting and coordination.

Without a general contractor, work flounders as the competing agendas of various laborers clash. The general contractor may or may not be skilled in carpentry, plumbing or electricity, but he or she is skilled in making sure the appropriate workers are in the right position at the right time.

Perhaps an additional image will add clarity: We don't hire a captain of a battleship and ask him to reenvision what the battleship does. We hire a captain to get the battleship to do what it was made to do.

In youth ministry, we've found that the typical general contractor is often a parent or at least someone a bit older than the laborers. The general contractor youth worker is typically high on organizational skills and does a good deal of work behind the scenes to make sure that events and programs run efficiently.

One warning: Because the general contractor for a youth ministry plays a key role in setting its climate, it's imperative that he or she be more than just organized. Many churches end up hiring highly anxious, highly defensive people into the general contractor role, just because the potential candidate is "highly organized." Such types often try to do all the work themselves, which usually multiplies the negativity. The most effective general contractors bring with them a calm playfulness and joy that has a way of profoundly infecting the climate of a youth ministry.

It isn't unusual for a church to hire a general contractor type and then expect him or her to demonstrate skill as a laborer, to be the creative, entertaining kid-magnet like the youth director at the church down the street. We've seen churches bounce between hiring a general contractor (who doesn't work out because the kids want someone younger) and the fun laborer (who doesn't work out because essential details keep getting dropped) with dizzying consistency.

3. The architect in the trailer. This is someone trained and experienced in designing the plans for a building, someone available throughout the building process to troubleshoot strategic challenges that inevitably arise.

On every large construction site sits a trailer with a large table on which blueprints can be spread and reviewed, a place for meeting with the architect who makes periodic visits to the site. The architect may or may not be skilled as a builder. Instead he or she makes sure the plan is followed, so the building will last beyond the departure of the beloved contractors and laborers.

The architect is the person who holds up construction until the plans are complete, the person who makes sure the workers don't waste time, money and energy building something that will later fall apart or, worse yet, have to be torn down to build it right the next time. This is the person who lays out the scope and sequence of the work (a sequence managed by the general contractor and carried out by the craftspeople) and who has experience handling the predictable surprises that are a part of every building project.

The architect brings a broad range of contacts, enough to ensure that the right person is hired at the right time. He or she brings a specific kind of competency, described by Jim Collins and Jerry Porras in their classic book, *Built to Last,* using the metaphor of a "time teller" and a "clock maker." A time teller has the skills to use available resources and technology available. A clock maker, on the other hand, knows how to build the timepiece from scratch. When a youth ministry hires a time teller and expects that person to be a clock maker, frustration is the predictable result.

In the typical youth ministry, churches simply assume that the craftsperson or the general contractor will take on all design responsibilities. As a result, most youth ministries are Scotch-taped and paper-clipped together.

A strategic church looks for an architect for its youth ministry first. The architect helps the stakeholders come to a consensus on their vision for the youth ministry and then draws up the plans for building it. Throughout the building process (typically a year to eighteen months), the architect ensures that all the right players are in place and keeps a finger on the pulse of the progress being made.

But the youth ministry architect need not be in a full-time, permanent position. I play this role at my church part-time. And our Youth Ministry Architect team plays this role for all the churches we work with.

Actually, having a full-time architect on a youth staff is no more necessary than having a permanent, full-time architect on the staff of a building project. The architect's role will be heavy on the front end of the process and then transition to a more strategic, troubleshooting, maintenance role after the ministry is up and running.

Though there are a few veteran youth workers who can play all three roles at the same time, a church's best chance at building a sustainable youth ministry will be to have three different people, each playing his or her position well. Though in some churches, volunteers will need to carry one or more of these roles, our experience is that defining the positions in this way dramatically maximizes a church's ability to build a sustainable youth ministry. There are obvious advantages:

- It allows youth ministry to be a training ground for the inexperienced, drastically reducing the possibility of the premature burnout of those with lifelong calls to ministry.

- It allows each successive youth worker to see himself or herself as a part of a team, in partnership not only with those who share current responsibility, but also with those who *have been* and *will be* a part of the building process for the very same youth ministry.

- It provides for a progression in the training of youth workers, as they move from simply *doing* the work to coordinating the work to designing the work.

- It provides a church with a long-term senior architect who ensures continuity and structural integrity and who becomes a resource for an annual strategic audit.

INOCULATION AGAINST STUPIDITY: SURVIVAL TIPS FOR SEARCH TEAMS

The church had spent almost a year searching for its next youth director. Though the search committee interviewed some candidates multiple times, they weren't excited about any of them. After that, potential candidates trickled in slowly.

As the church moved closer to the one-year anniversary of their youth director's departure, they became increasingly anxious. Though the ministry was continuing to move forward with steady, if slow, momentum, the search committee was getting tired. They simply couldn't imagine starting over again. They *had* to hire *someone*. As one member of the church admitted later, "We wound up hiring the best of all the people we didn't want."

> You're better off hiring temporary help or holding back expansion plans than you are rushing this process. . . . It's more expensive to keep hiring, training, and losing recent seminary graduates than it is to just offer a larger salary to someone with a proven track record.
>
> MIKE WOODRUFF

It wasn't long after the new youth director stepped onto the scene that folks began to wonder if they'd made a mistake. As kids began voting with their feet, parental complaints multiplied like rabbits. Within two years, the new youth worker—clearly gifted, but a mismatch for this church—left devastated and defeated.

By some estimates, a bad church hire can cost a church as much as forty thousand dollars. But the cost of a bad hire is so much more than financial, puncturing the sense of call of the mismatched staff person, deflating the momentum of a youth ministry, erasing the trust of students.

For all kinds of reasons, it makes sense to get it right the first time.

We've often observed that those responsible for a search frequently step into the process with two strikes against them:

1. It's likely that no one on the team has ever been a part of the search for a professional youth worker before.

2. Some members of the search team will come with a particular axe to

grind—wanting to make sure that the next hire is spiritual enough or fun enough or mature enough.

As a result, most search teams make almost all the same mistakes.

SO YOU WANT TO HIRE A YOUTH MINISTER? DON'T FOLLOW ME.

I've tried to imagine what sadder-but-wiser search teams might say if they could give us their best advice. I imagine that their handbook might contain the following kinds of information:

The people you hire will do what they like to do, so hire people who like to do the things the job requires. Not long ago, youth ministry guru Dean Trulear described to me the difference between skills and tal-

> The bolder our plans, the more competent the people we attract.
>
> MIKE WOODRUFF

ents. Talents, he explained, are like writing with our dominant hand. Skills, on the other hand, are like writing with our nondominant hand. The research he shared shows that if a person's job requires that more than 40 percent of his or her time be spent on skills (work that doesn't access talents), that person will never thrive in the job.

Far too many youth directors avoid the tasks that are central to success in their jobs. For instance, an amazing number of youth directors have a hard time spending time actually with kids—not all kids, mind you, just the kids they aren't comfortable with. Other youth workers feel intimidated talking to adults, the very people they need as partners if they are to build a sustainable ministry. And the vast majority of youth workers we know simply can't find the time to look beyond this week's lesson.

Hiring the right person has little to do with his or her youth ministry theory. Whether a candidate believes in an "emergent" or "family-based" or "purpose-driven" philosophy has little to do with his or her ability to do the job effectively. The best test of what a future youth worker will do is what he or she has done, or at least what he or she loves to do.

If you don't know where your youth ministry is going, the new staff person will take it somewhere else. Search committees that wait for their new youth ministers to tell them where the ministry should go are setting themselves (and the future staff) up for failure.

I was finishing seminary when I was interviewed for my current position. As the pastor and I headed for the airport, he said the words that totally closed the deal for me: "If you come here, you will have *carte blanche.* You can bring *your* vision and build this program the way you would want it to look."

To an eager twenty-seven-year-old who didn't know how much he didn't know, that heady invitation was too much to resist. More than anything, I wanted to be in charge (though I would have been loathe to admit it at the time), to create the ministry I wanted, to try out all the ideas I'd been studying and generating for the past few years.

But if I'd stayed in my position for the 3.9-year average (there was a quiet little mob who would have been happy to see me go by the 3.9-year point), I'm certain I would have handed the ministry to my successor in a bigger mess than I received it.

Here's what I've learned: The church didn't need me to tell them what *my* vision for youth ministry should be. The church needed someone who could help the congregation discover its own vision.

Organizational expert Michael Gerber suggests that hiring organizations not even announce their job openings until they've written an operations manual of "the way we do it around here." He goes on to give a surprising description of the person most organizations should be looking for:

- "Not a Master Technician. But a novice. A beginner. An apprentice."

- "Someone for whom questions haven't become answers."

- "Someone who is open to the possibility of learning skills he hasn't developed yet, skills he wants to learn."

Be honest about numbers. When Doug Fields asked parents in his church what they were looking for in a youth director, he received forty very different expectations. He notes only two in common:

1. Grow the group.

2. Create a youth ministry the students will enjoy.

Make no mistake about it. Almost every youth worker will be expected to cause the ministry to grow. And almost every youth worker will face the expectation that he or she will create a ministry that students *want* to come to.

To tell a youth ministry candidate, "Our church is not concerned about numbers," though perhaps well-meaning, is dishonest and unfair to the person being interviewed. An effective committee communicates growth expectations clearly. If they can't agree on what those are, they're not ready to begin the search (do not pass go; do not collect two hundred dollars; do not make the first query call).

If you want someone to stay, find some way to pay. A decade or so ago, the average full-time youth worker's salary was $26,625 (including those with decades of experience). But figure 6 gives us more recent averages.

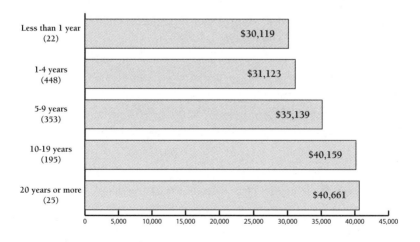

Figure 6. Median Salary by Years of Experience—Job: Youth Pastor (United States) (Data provided by PayScale, Inc. © www.payscale.com)

A church (intentionally or unintentionally) communicates how long it wants its staff to stay by how much it's willing to pay. Of course, ministry is not just about dollars and cents, but what we pay our staff does say something about how we value them. Too many churches pay new youth workers at a level that, as soon as they become experienced enough to be effective and old enough to start a family, the only way they can earn enough is by moving to another church—or out of youth ministry altogether.

We offer churches the following general rules in identifying normal youth ministry salary patterns (not including the cost of benefits):

- $25,000 to $35,000—a youth worker with little or no experience, whom you expect to remain in his or her position for three years or less

- $35,000 to $50,000—a youth worker who has proven effectiveness in a previous ministry

- $50,000 to $75,000—a youth worker who will be expected to hire, train and supervise other staff, in addition to recruiting and equipping twenty-five or more volunteers

Of course, the real dollar amount may vary widely in different parts of the country, but these figures can give search teams a reasonable starting point. In addition to salary, a church will want to consider the less tangible value of benefits such as car or travel allowance, continuing education, pension or retirement contributions, professional supplies or book allowance, and health insurance.

If you want your youth worker to succeed, define what "success" will look like. Most youth workers think they've been hired to build relationships with students and develop creative programs. Few realize they've been hired to run a complex organization.

No one told them that they were not only in charge of developing the program but of marketing it as well. No one told them they were not only responsible for building relationships with students but also for building a team that makes sure someone is building a relationship with *every* student.

Seldom do unspoken expectations rear their heads in the context of a calm, clarifying discussion. Most often they come in the form of multiplying complaints that leave the youth worker feeling as if he or she was lied to somewhere in the interview process.

Search teams do candidates a favor when they're clear about the standards they use to measure progress. The standard doesn't need to be limited to the number of youth attending programs. It can include less bottom-line-driven metrics like

- How many people's names is the youth worker expected to know?

- How often is the youth worker expected to be in contact with every youth and every family?

- How many volunteers do we expect the youth worker to recruit and train?

- How many hours of "face time" does the church expect the youth worker to have with students?

- How many times a year is at least one person from the church expected to be in touch with a typical student?

The best way to protect a new staff person from the chaos resulting from "terminal vagueness" is to make expectations as clear as crystal.

A NEW KIND OF SUPERSTAR

Though transition is part and parcel of managing a sustainable youth ministry, seldom is any thought given to what sort of long-term infrastructure will be put in place to prevent the new staff person's eventual departure from creating widespread panic. As in basketball, the game of youth ministry is won or lost in the transitions.

As strange as it may sound, over and over again we have seen youth ministries we work with actually *gain* momentum during an interim period because the appropriate systems are in place.

When we hire the least experienced to do some of the most complex and challenging work in the church, a high casualty rate is predictable.

When a church chronically underinvests in youth ministry and expects Superman results from a Clark Kent youth director, it should not surprise us when that youth worker leaves the job less passionate about the call to ministry than when he or she first arrived.

But what would happen if more churches felt called to cultivate—not just find—superstars? What would happen if churches spent time creating an intentional process that would maximize the possibility that their current, young, inexperienced staff would, one day, become the kind of superstar (not just in youth ministry, but in their homes and their personal lives as well) every church seems to be looking for?

In addition, many of the most effective leaders in today's churches had significant experience in effective youth ministry before moving into senior leadership. Sustainable youth ministry is a fertile training ground for well-equipped, effective leaders for the larger church.

What would happen if churches saw the cultivation of *this* kind of superstar as central to their calling?

8

ALIGNING THE HEART

The Emotionally Healthy Youth Worker

Nothing is going to change . . . until you and I figure out what is wrong with the person in the mirror.

DONALD MILLER

It is not possible for a Christian to be spiritually mature while remaining emotionally immature.

PETER SCAZZERO

Above all else, guard your heart,
*   for it is the wellspring of life.*

PROVERBS 4:23

Sadly, the longer you are in youth ministry, the longer your list of sidelined and flatlined comrades becomes. And the obvious question is Why?

MIKE HIGGS

Little did I know about the monster that decided to tag along on my first mission trip to Mexico.

I was barely twenty years old, serving as an assistant youth director, deeply committed to being "radical for Christ," to pushing kids out of their comfort zone. I made it a point on the trip to meet with kids individually to challenge them in their discipleship, to pray with them, to push them to never settle for less than God's best in their lives.

Though we worked in one-hundred-degree heat every day, most mornings I led a group of our most committed students on a predawn jog for a few miles (after waking from four to five hours of sleep to have my own quiet time first). Each night, we'd go to a local park and do children's ministry, as well as have time together as a group. Leading fifty kids or so, traveling around Mexico on an old church bus (which I often drove) and keeping the kids motivated to work (many seemed to require my perpetual prodding) made for ten very intense days. But I loved every minute of it.

Well, almost every minute.

In our evenings at the park, the guys in the group would throw together a quick, full-contact football game (as if we needed more exercise!). And each night, I would line up against the same guy. He was much bigger and more muscular than I was and he seemed to enjoy the opportunity to throw me to the ground, play after infuriating play.

On the last night of the trip, when we had returned to our football ritual, things had moved from frustrating to tense, as I found myself flat on my back on each successive play. Returning to the line of scrimmage for what would be the last time that night, my gridiron adversary gave the slightest smirk across the line. And when the ball was snapped, so did I.

I jumped across the line with arms flailing, fists searching for any target I could find on my tormentor. As slack-jawed kids watched my demonstration of Christian love in action, I yelled a few angry words at my opponent and stormed off.

At least it wasn't a kid I was attacking.

Or a parent.

It was just my boss.

He pulled me aside and took me on a long walk, as slowly, very slowly, I calmed down.

I would like to say that a light bulb went off in my head at that moment, and I immediately realized that, physically and emotionally, I was a powder keg ready to explode. But instead I chose to focus on my boss's pugilistic pummelings, rather than deal with my own unhealthy pattern, my lack of self-care and boundaries, a drivenness I excused in the name of being wildly committed to following Christ.

THE COST OF IGNORING OUR OWN HEARTS

We simply cannot build a healthy, sustainable youth ministry on the backs of those who are not healthy themselves. Peter Scazzero was right when he wrote in *The Emotionally Healthy Church,* "The overall health of any church or ministry depends primarily on the emotional and spiritual health of its leadership." We may be able to build "dynamic" ministries, "magnetic" ministries, even "radical, sold-out, on-fire" ministries without it, but not healthy or sustainable ones.

The youth and parents at Al's church discovered this principle with crushing clarity. In the five years Al worked as a youth director for Eastside Church, he turned his youth group from floundering to fabulous. And fifteen years or so after his departure, he had become legendary, larger than life in the memory of many parents and young adults in the church. In focus groups, person after person affirmed, "If only we could get another Al. Now *he* was amazing!"

But over a decade later, Al's church was still languishing in a post-hero stall, hoping against hope that their next hire would live up to their dream of "another Al." Though the church had gone through a series of youth workers, none ever got close to the high bar set by Al.

But five years after Al's departure, the church received staggering news that stopped them in their tracks, news that, at first, they refused to believe was even possible: Al had taken his own life.

When I heard this story, I had to wonder, what if Al's "success" was part of the problem? More to the point, what if Al died from the toxic combination of a church culture with extraordinarily high expectations and his own willingness to sacrifice his emotional health to meet those expectations? I began to ask myself if there is something in the chemistry of some churches that rewards those who produce a highly visible ministry, even at the cost of their imploding lives.

Sadly, we frequently find ourselves working in youth ministries in the wake of youth workers who spent almost all their time investing in ministry and little to no time tending to their own hearts. We've heard a litany of tragedy—broken families, addiction, embezzlement, pornography, prison terms and suicide— enough evidence to show a clear pattern of once-revered high producers who, it was later revealed, had busily built their ministries over a crater in their own hearts.

> **What gets sacrificed in the busyness of youth ministry is not our "to do list" but our hearts.**
>
> DOUG FIELDS

I'm not suggesting for a second that the men and women I've just described did not love God. I'm not suggesting that they weren't people of prayer, that they weren't fully devoted to following Christ. I'm not suggesting that they led ministries that didn't "work." In fact, just the opposite seems to be true.

Most of them are remembered in their churches for their phenomenal visible results. Kids loved them for their ubiquitous availability. Parents loved them for their people pleasing. Church leaders loved them for their workaholic tendencies. What I'm suggesting is that in their pursuit of a successful ministry they forfeited the most important asset they had to bring to their kids: the integrity of their own souls.

On one list of concerns of professional youth ministers, the number-one response was "feelings of personal inadequacy." Those of us who do ministry from a foundation of inadequacy can be driven to grow our groups to bolster our own confidence. We get angry with parents who don't cooperate with our compulsion to find our worth in their children showing up at our programs. We blame our students for their lack of "commitment" when they aren't willing to miss a soccer tournament for a youth retreat.

The church can no longer afford to hire eager young adults who know very little about themselves. We can no longer afford to assume that solutions to youth ministry problems lie in placing the entire weight of a ministry on an enthusiastic leader's shoulders. Because youth ministry, like every ministry, is life-on-life, *we reproduce who we are,* and the fissures in our own heart are only magnified in the ministries we build.

HARD IS . . . WELL . . . HARD

The young youth worker looked across the table at me, tears brimming. "This is *hard*," he said with understated clarity. He had stepped into his youth director position with the absolute confidence that only the inexperienced know. After six months, he sat before me a broken man. The combination of an intensely anxious church climate and his own defensive spirit had driven him to the pavement again and again, leaving him seeing no option but to turn in his resignation, a decision he made soon after our conversation.

> There was a kind of sad gaiety about the way they went about their work. The sadness stemmed, I suppose, from the hopelessness of their task—the problems were so vast, their resources for dealing with them were so meager—and the gaiety from a hope beyond hope that, in the long run if not the short all would some holy and unimaginable way be well.
>
> FREDERICK BUECHNER

Sometimes by their own complicity, sometimes by the unhealthy expectations of the multiple constituencies they serve, sometimes simply by being caught innocently in political crossfire, enough youth workers star in their own church horror stories to convince us that my young friend was right: this *is* hard.

Youth workers who don't feel over their heads, who don't feel they're overwhelmed and failing at times, may simply not understand their jobs. In fact, this recognition may be the first step in approaching youth ministry from an emotionally healthy place.

Julian of Norwich wrote that our wounds are not ends in themselves. She suggests that our wounds have a way of becoming a *womb* in which God's new creation can be birthed. I've heard some scholars suggest that Job was actually the first book of the Bible written, as if the first idea God wanted to communicate to his people was that this life is hard, that pain is real.

The emotionally healthy youth worker does not run from pain, but keeps his or her eyes open to the ways that God is at work, even in the pain, transforming the fertile fields of brokenness into something entirely new.

FREEING THE VICTIM

The first step toward doing ministry out of emotional maturity is to take responsibility for our own emotional health. It begins when we recognize that our circumstances don't make us happy, sad, mad, ashamed or afraid; our circumstances simply reveal those emotions in us. Working from a place of emotional maturity happens when we know our hearts well enough to see the ways we're choosing our own stuckness.

> **The first step was always the most difficult: getting a young leader to recognize that before circumstances could change, *he* [or *she*] might have to change.**
>
> **ANDY STANLEY**

When we become stuck, our ministries can become stuck as well. In his work with thousands of small-business owners, Michael Gerber discovered,

> The "dream" is rarely realized; most small businesses fail. And the reason is obvious. *We bring our chaos with us.*
>
> We don't change. We try to change "out there." We try to change the world . . . but we stay the same.

Most of us would rather externalize our problems—an overcritical church, fanatically apathetic youth, too many expectations. But no lasting change can happen in our ministries until they happen first in us. In coaching youth workers, we have discovered that one of the first road-blocks we must overcome is the victim mentality, which has become epidemic among youth staff.

We hear victim catchphrases like, "The church won't let me . . ." and "My senior pastor just won't . . ." and "Our community has soccer practice on Sundays." If it's not the senior pastor, it's the elders. If it's not the bratty kids, it's their apathetic parents. If it's not the music minister, it's the women of the church, who always seem to have another volunteer project for the youth to do.

As true as these factors might be, this sort of thinking keeps youth workers in a victim state, trapped in emotional ruts. I'm not talking about denying that problems exist. I'm talking about facing those problems with brutal honesty, not just the problems "out there," but more importantly our own toxic tendency to become enmeshed in, defensive about or overwhelmed by those problems.

When we first met with Bob, he wore his anger like a tattoo on the forehead, obvious to everyone but him. When confronted with the defensiveness and anger he brought to almost every encounter, he quickly justified his negativity by pointing to "ridiculous" expectations or inconsistent behavior in those offering criticism.

Having been on the receiving end of intense and disproportionate criticism, Bob had chosen to localize his anger around his disappointment with the senior pastor, who "never backed me up." As we probed to find out the content issue, it became clear that this youth worker had a number of expectations for his senior pastor that were clearly not being met. We kept hearing one complaint over and over: "I've been here three years, and my boss has only once had a meeting with just me!"

I asked the obvious: "When is the last time you asked for an appointment?" Bob let me know, in no uncertain terms, that *his boss* needed to take the initiative to set up those kinds of meetings.

To move out of the victim role, Bob needed a shift in focus—away from what the senior pastor *wasn't* doing to what the youth pastor *could* do. We could have, of course, stayed mired in the debate about whose responsibility it *should* have been. But debating about who should take responsibility would only increase Bob's anger without moving him one step closer to what he wanted. If he wanted to have more-frequent one-on-one meetings with his senior pastor, he could (in fact, must) step out of the victim role and get on the pastor's calendar. We start doing ministry out of a place of emotional maturity when we take responsibility for our own schedule (and for our own defensiveness).

Too many youth workers step into ministry with a passion to change the world, a passion that, if harnessed and healthy, has the potential to draw us more deeply into the work God created us to do. But when we seek to change the world out of our compulsions, without being willing to face our demons, the changes left in our wake may be anything but holy.

GET A LIFE: THE ANATOMY OF EMOTIONAL
HEALTH IN MINISTRY

Those called to youth ministry often assume that if they're gifted in ministry, if there is visible fruit, they must be on the right track. Others assume that if they're spiritually disciplined, theologically trained or well informed in their fields, they have sufficient emotional health to sustain themselves in ministry for the long haul. But it doesn't take many years of observation to recognize that there's simply no correlation between giftedness for ministry and the emotional maturity to manage it.

Without appropriate boundaries, without intentional habits of self-restoration, without accountable and intimate relationships, none of us is equipped to carry on a healthy and sustainable ministry for long. As I shared some of these principles recently with the students at the Center for Youth Ministry Training in Nashville, a young woman asked the very logical question, "So *how* do we do that?"

I've given a good bit of thought to Jill's question and have developed a few of my own in response, questions designed to help those of us in ministry do our work from a place of emotional maturity.

Do I have a life outside ministry? Our ministry will be severely limited if we bring to it little more than our obsessive focus on ministry. If we have little or no life apart from ministry, we can easily have unrealistic expectations of our colleagues and the organization we serve.

Eventually, we simply become a faint (and boring) echo of what the ministry already is.

I was fascinated to learn from Michigan State University's Robert Root-Bernstein's research that Nobel Prize winners and most members of the National Academy of Sciences were "universally artistic and/or musical, most had several arts-related hobbies as adults and they utilized a wide range of arts-associated mental thinking tools such as three-dimensional imagery, kinesthetic feelings and pattern formation." The research also discovered that "high aptitude in arts and music [is] much more predictive of career success in any field than the results of grades, IQ, achievement or any other standardized measure."

When we have little or no life outside our ministries, we can easily develop unrealistic expectations, thinking that the church should "parent" us, provide a close circle of friends for us, offer worship and teaching stimulating enough that we always "get something out of it." But when we have a life outside work, we approach our imperfect institutions with a peace that can lead to long-term change. When I begin to take myself and my situation too seriously, it helps to remember that, in the animal world, it's the most intelligent creatures that play.

Do I have an emotionally healthy schedule? Emotional health does not come automatically. What does come automatically is the pursuit of our own compulsions. We don't naturally step out of the need to be needed, the need to be perfect, the need to be special, the need to win, the need to be wise. Instead we assume our compulsions are allies, and too often we follow them with blind, passionate obedience.

Though there are many things we can do to stay emotionally healthy, one of the most universal among those who lead sustainable youth ministries is a habit we call the "rhythmic week." Here's the way the rhythmic week looks for one of our full-time clients:

	Sunday	Monday	Tuesday	Wednesday	Thursday	Friday	Saturday
Morning	Program time		Balcony time	Personal time	Sabbath	Flex time	Flex time
Afternoon	Flex time				Sabbath		Flex time
Evening	Program time	Personal time	Flex time	Program time	Sabbath	Contract work	Personal time

Figure 7.

The blank sections are the time when the youth worker goes at full speed. Sabbath and personal time are protected times—to be intentionally away from work. Flex times could be designated either for work or for time off, depending on the demands of the week. (See the description of balcony time in the next chapter.)

The rhythmic week begins with the discipline of the Sabbath. Regardless of how many hours we pack into a week, the habit of one full day of rest each week makes a huge difference in our emotional health, often preventing us from being emotionally driven or emotionally empty.

Interestingly, the vast majority of youth ministers we've worked with were not taking a full Sabbath day each week. Some even laughed at the idea of a day off, as if it were a luxury for someone with less important work to do (this, in spite of the fact that the whole idea of the Sabbath comes just one commandment away from the prohibition against murder).

Young people need youth workers who have God— rather than youth ministry— first and foremost in view.

MIKE KING

When we fail to keep our bodies in the rhythm they were designed with, we reveal what we really believe about ministry: that the work of transformation is up to us, not God. Like anxious gardeners trying to force plants out of seeds, instead of cultivating change, we kill the very seeds that were meant to produce change.

I'm not talking about a reactionary legalism. I'm talking about practicing the rhythm God designed for our bodies, the rhythm of six days of work and one day of rest. Those who fail to practice Sabbath or other disciplines of emotional health become victims of their job descriptions rather than architects of them.

Remember the story of the goose who laid the golden eggs? The impatient owner of the goose decided he simply didn't have time to wait for the egg to be laid, so he killed the goose to get immediate access to the gold. Reminds me of the way many churches treat their youth workers.

One of the most important lessons I had to learn as a youth pastor was that one of the greatest gifts I can bring to my ministry is myself. If I sacrifice my joy in Christ or my passion for the gospel on the altar of "successful ministry," everybody loses. As a dear brother in ministry told me just after his divorce, "If you sacrifice your family for your ministry, no one will ever thank you for it."

If I don't take care of the goose, no one else will. I've tried to manipulate others into taking care of me, sometimes by "sharing" how exhausted I was or how much pressure I was under and other times by trying to be so helpful to others that they'd eventually return the favor and take care of me. But those strategies never work for long.

We don't have to wait until the goose is nearly dead to do something. Every now and then, the emotionally healthy youth worker must do a "goose check," and if the goose is getting sick, he or she must find help nursing the heart of the goose back to health.

How much do I know about what I don't know? Jim Collins suggests, "Great decisions begin with really great people and a simple statement: I don't know." Godly leaders approach problems, whether in the ministry or in themselves, with a curious humility, recognizing just how much they don't know.

When youth ministries fail, it's not because their leaders don't know enough about small groups, organizational leadership, relationship building or developing volunteers. Those things can be learned. Youth

> Our controlled frenzy creates the illusion of a well-ordered existence. We move from crisis to crisis, responding to the urgent and neglecting the essential. We still walk around. We still perform all the gestures and actions identified as human, but we resemble people carried along on the mechanical sidewalk at the airport. The fire in the belly dies. We no longer hear what Boris Pasternak called "the inward music" of our belovedness.
>
> BRENNAN MANNING

ministers fail because, instead of investing the effort to learn something new, they spend their energy defending what they think they already know. The first step is self-awareness, acknowledging—day after day—how much there is to learn.

Our team has assisted with enough transitions and tracked the effectiveness and tenure of those hires enough to recognize that the most counterproductive hire in youth ministry is the one who brings a spirit of anxiousness and defensiveness. I'm not talking about the natural jitters that come in a job interview. Rather, I'm talking about a pervading spirit the anxious person brings into a room.

With few filters for what criticism to pay attention to and what criticism to ignore, these anxious youth workers ward off would-be "attackers" with tears, defensiveness, "facts," anger and preemptive attacks that discredit those who might bring complaints. Because the anxious person may be capable of cranking out a lot of work, churches are easily wooed into hiring this kind of person.

Anxious youth workers also bring one unignorable deficit: they seldom have the time (or the orientation) to build a team, to manage a system. They often work at a feverish pace, which is initially celebrated by those who, from a distance, observe the immediate impact on the program. Though anxious leaders may ask people to help, they seldom, if ever, ask for partners.

When we first met Louise, the young, overwhelmed youth worker at a church we were working with, we hoped she could give us a quick picture of the lay of the land, some clue to what had kept this youth ministry faltering for the past few years. Our conversation went something like this:

YMA: "Tell us about participation. Has there—"

Lousie (interrupting): "I've been trying to get an accurate list for years, and nobody seems to know how to do it. We've got kids on the list who haven't been here for years. People will tell you that they had seventy-five kids coming to youth group every week five years ago, when I was just a volunteer. But I was here then. There is no way we had seventy-five kids. We might have had forty-five, maybe even peaked at sixty at one time. But we didn't have seventy-five kids."

YMA: "How many—" [intending to ask, "How many kids would the church like to see involved?"]

Louise: "I'm not a big numbers person. I just don't believe you can judge a program by numbers. This past week, I met with a young man, Jimmy, whose mom committed suicide six weeks ago. You can't measure the impact of what we are doing in his life. You can't count it. It doesn't fit on a spreadsheet or a tracking system somewhere."

YMA: "So let's talk about volunteers. Who are—"

Louise: "This is just not a church that knows how to volunteer. In the church I grew up in—now *that* church could volunteer. But it's like these people will write a check but they don't want to get their hands dirty. It's been a problem ever since I've been here, and every staff person will tell you the same thing."

Though Louise didn't answer a single one of our questions, she told us volumes about the anxious climate she was bringing to the youth ministry.

Anxious people are notoriously un-self-aware. They easily overcommit and often attempt to manipulate those around them into pity about how much they have to do. They typically have so little ability to say no that when they do say it, they say it with such harshness that people are taken aback. Though most of our clients are grateful for the soul-tending work we do with them, the anxious ones have a much harder time receiving this sort of care.

Have you ever had the experience of walking into a room with a strong odor and asking someone working in that space, "How can you handle these fumes?" only to hear the quizzical response, "What fumes?"

Knowing how easy it is to be oblivious to those things about us that are obvious to others, the emotionally healthy youth worker takes time to build relationships with wise and faithful friends who will speak the truth—counselors, spiritual directors, older friends in ministry. When we spend almost all our time with those less self-aware than we are (that is, teenagers), we're inviting stagnation in our own growth.

Emotionally healthy youth workers protect themselves from self-delusion by learning what their gifts are not, by admitting their blind-spots and the triggers that create defensiveness or avoidance. They know their own family-system stories enough to know the roles they easily fall into, roles like the hero, the scapegoat, the clown and the lost child, roles they learned in childhood as a key to survival and success.

When we don't know our own brokenness and the games we play to get what we want, we live out this principle: "The person who hurts the most causes the most pain." Emotionally healthy leaders have a hunger to learn, not just about ministry but also about themselves; they may not know what they're doing—in ministry, in marriage, in managing their own heart—but they care enough to find out.

Do I rule my tongue, or does it rule me? Youth ministry is a breeding ground for sarcasm. Quick-witted youth workers can protect themselves from their feelings of inadequacy by being quicker with a putdown than the cockiest junior-high boy. Jeanne Mayo warns,

> I've known many "cool" youth leaders who have become special-ists at communicating with teenagers through sarcasm. Ironically, the students they feel the most connected to are often the ones who get the brunt of their verbal jabs. The youth leader, who doesn't realize what he or she is doing, thinks, "The student knows I'm only joking. I kid with him that way because I really like him." Yet Proverbs 26:18-19 describes this behavior in a less than glamorous light: "Like a madman shooting firebrands or deadly arrows is a man who deceives his neighbor and says, 'I was only joking!'"

Whom do I take more seriously—God or myself? Most churches (and many youth pastors) take themselves very seriously, often so seriously that they completely miss the foolishness of their obsessive focus on petty problems within their church. The king of Lilliput in *Gulliver's Travels* comes to mind.

I was with a group of youth pastors recently, at what I can only describe as a "preach off." This was a first gathering of men and women who had never met before, and like strutting bulls, each wanted to "declare war" on the evil in our city. As we went around the table introducing ourselves, the bravado got louder and the evils got uglier, as each leader spouted the unique and explosive ways they would be transforming the city. I was there just to have lunch with others who know how lonely and hard this work can be.

Too often, we reveal how we avoid taking God seriously by showing how seriously we take our ministries and ourselves. I remember when one of my colleagues left her ministry at our church. After six months, we happened to see each other. During our visit, she said something fascinating: "I discovered exactly what the rest of our city thinks about our church." I was eager to hear what she had seen from "the real world." She said simply (and I believe accurately), "It never crosses their minds!"

Emotionally healthy youth workers have escaped the illusion that the weight of transforming their cities and churches is on their shoulders. Because they've learned not to take themselves too seriously, when criticized they can simply say, "I'm sorry"—period, with no excuses or casting of blame. They can live with a failed program and stalled momentum, give their best, and trust God with the results.

What am I fighting about? Some youth workers seem determined to take the hard way, to find something to fight about, even when a better, clearer way is obvious. I'm reminded of the story of the old bull and the young bull (slightly adapted):

> There was once an old bull and a young bull grazing in the pasture. On the other side of the fence were hundreds of apples, a favorite snack of bulls. The young bull strutted and said to the old bull, "Whadya say we break through that fence over there and eat one of those apples?"
>
> The old bull continued to chew his cud slowly, began walking and said, "Whadya say we go down to that open gate, walk through it and eat *all* those apples?"

Emotionally healthy youth workers aren't afraid to continue to name a problem or to disagree when conscience dictates it, but they are able to be assertive without being aggressive. They're able to stay engaged (they don't storm out of the room) without becoming enmeshed (taking every disagreement as a personal attack). They have more in their conflict management toolbox than fight or flight.

What do I do after I fail? Hitting the wall can result in one of two responses. Either we keep doing what we've been doing, banging our heads against the same wall until we give up in defeat, blaming ourselves and everyone around us. Or we get curious. We find people who are accomplishing the things we're failing to accomplish, and we ask for advice. We find out what effective people do and imitate those things until we get the same results.

It's easy to assume that people who are thriving where we are failing are just "better," more gifted, maybe even "lucky." But from the nonanxious perch, it's not difficult to see that these people are simply doing different things than we are doing (and thus getting different results).

Is no a four-letter word to me? Many of us have a hard time saying no. Some have trouble saying no to just one more appointment or one more text message or one more phone call. Others have trouble saying no to just one more video game, one more cheeseburger or one more look at an illicit photograph.

But if we are to say a clear yes to the unique vocation God has given us, we must be willing to say no to lots of other things. We must embrace the fact that *no* is not a dirty word and that we will disappoint someone when we say it. As Tony Robinson said, "Leadership is learning to disappoint people at a rate they can handle."

Youth workers who aren't able to say the clear, nonanxious no on the

> **Transformations come only as we go the long way round, only as we're willing to walk a different, longer, more arduous, more inward, more prayerful route.**
>
> SUE MONK KIDD

front end often wind up responding to requests with harsh, melodramatic comments like "I just can't sacrifice my family anymore!" when a simple "I won't be able to make that meeting" will do.

Am I burning out or just burning? There's one difference between a candle and an oil lantern: the wick in a candle burns *itself* as the wax disappears. But the wick in an oil lantern preserves itself by burning the oil first. The wick begins to burn only when the oil is completely gone. Emotionally healthy youth workers ensure that the reservoir of oil in their lamps is full.

Most youth workers are thermometers; they can tell you the temperature of their ministry. But they often fail to be thermostats, influencing the temperature of that ministry. They feel powerless to catalyze change, to create climate rather than simply react to it. Of course, the most powerful resource we have for creating lasting change is to initiate change in ourselves first.

Emotional health in ministry begins with being willing to take a hard look at ourselves and to do the courageous and often uncomfortable work of attending to our own hearts.

> **The world is full of people who are waiting for someone to come along and motivate them to be the kind of people they wish they could be. The problem is that no one is coming. . . . These people are waiting for a bus on a street where no busses pass. . . . They can end up waiting forever. And that is what most people do.**
>
> BRIAN TRACY

9

MONKEYS, FROGS AND BALCONIES

Secrets of Third-Pig Youth Workers

He who every morning plans the transactions of the day and follows out that plan carries a thread that will guide him through the labyrinth of the most busy life. . . . But where no plan is laid, where the disposal of time is surrendered merely to the chance of incident, chaos will soon reign.

VICTOR HUGO

[T]he men of Issachar . . . understood the times and knew what Israel should do.

1 CHRONICLES 12:32

Every time I'm tempted to leave my church for greener pastures, I do the math. Now that I've been in the same church for more than twenty years, certain things come easier: recruiting, fundraising, promotion. In my early years here, I had to work twice as hard to get a fraction of the current results, because I didn't understand the invisible systems.

Today there is momentum—momentum from years of moving intentionally in the same direction. As I do the math, I realize it would take me twenty years to get to exactly the same place at another church. By then, I'd be seventy.

Maybe it's my math skills that keep me staying put.

Or maybe it's just that I've seen enough youth workers crushed by the delusion that getting out of their current "dysfunctional" church will make everything all right again.

MAKING LONGEVITY LIKELY

Longevity simply works—on all kinds of levels. It forces us to face up to the patterns *within ourselves* that keep our youth ministries less than effective. It forces us to continue relating to people who have let us down. In a world of disposable relationships, longevity creates a durable Christian community that keeps on loving in spite of disappointments, failures and manipulation. Longevity gives us the chance to learn from our mistakes and to do our part to build it better the next time around.

But longevity isn't easy. My first five or six years at my current church almost killed me. But as I passed the seven-year threshold, something happened. I started to observe movement I didn't initiate; I began to see our ministry carried along by a momentum that had been slowly, imperceptibly building for years.

Maybe this is why, according to one expert, "No church in America has sustained a large youth ministry [200 plus] without long-term ten-

> Youth ministry is littered with people who bail out as soon as a bit of water comes over the bow. . . . Changing this church for the next one means trading problems that you know about for problems that that you don't know about. And besides, wherever you end up, you'll still be there, which guarantees that most of the same problems will be there too.
>
> MIKE WOODRUFF

ure in its ministry DNA." In addition, both the level of satisfaction and the level of effectiveness in ministry dramatically increase with tenure. And ironically, it's the long-term youth worker who is best positioned to build a youth ministry *not* dependent on him or her.

The largest statistical study of the profession of youth ministry concluded with this counsel to youth workers:

> Persevere. The longer you minister with youth, the more goals you will see accomplished, the more competent and confident you will feel, the more satisfaction you will derive from your relationships with youth and their parents and the stronger will be your sense of purpose and confidence in God and his Word.

Longevity is a great idea, but for reasons very different than we might think. A well-intentioned mother offered this comment about the importance of longevity in youth leaders:

> My daughter—an active member of the youth group—has bonded with and then had to say goodbye to three different youth ministers over the years. How do you teach a teenager about perseverance and the importance of long, committed relationships when your church life can't back it up? How do you deal with the hurt and hesitation of building new relationships when they keep falling away?

Her questions reveal a common yet fatal assumption about youth workers—namely, that the *key relationships* in youth ministry are those built between the professional and the student. It's actually the *unhealthy* ministry that pivots around the youth worker's ability to build relationships with every student. In this sort of youth ministry, relationships with other Christian adults are considered second-rate.

There's nothing inherently wrong or trust-breaking about kids having short-term relationships with godly adults. Most kids have little trouble bonding deeply with camp counselors with whom they spend only a few days or weeks. When our kids return from camp, we don't wring our hands, saying, "How can my child ever trust again, after having built strong relationships with so many different counselors at camp?"

No, the value of a camp is not limited because of the presence or absence of different leaders—in fact, it is enhanced. The good camp—like a healthy youth ministry—involves a constellation of relationships, and a good camp counselor—like a good youth worker—simply adds to that constellation.

The problem is not turnover in staff. The problem is in the culture of churches that assume the only way to sustainability in youth ministry is to hire a youth worker who will stay for decades.

I'm not suggesting that high turnover is inherently good. What I'm suggesting is that the more intentional a church is at building a sustainable youth ministry, the more likely it is that its staff will choose to stay for the long haul. Longevity does not happen by chance. It is undeniably impacted by the overall climate of the youth ministry. Churches with youth ministries that are appropriately funded and that have clear, measurable expectations tend to have momentum, and staff members just tend to stay longer.

But in churches where the structure and goals are fuzzy or where each successive youth worker is expected to build the ministry from scratch, youth workers are much more likely to become entangled in conflict. And conflict turns out to be, far and away, the number-one reason youth workers give for leaving.

Far too many youth workers find themselves moving on much sooner than expected. Over the years we've stumbled onto a few curiously named habits that seem to be built into the DNA of youth workers who stay for the long haul. We always start with eating frogs.

EAT THAT FROG

Not long ago, Dave Rahn and his colleagues at the Link Institute sought to identify the greatest challenges facing professional youth workers. After surveying thousands, they identified the five most challenging issues:

1. When busy, I sacrifice my devotional time.

2. The job demands are more than time allows.

3. I feel the emotional strain of my work.

4. I regret not spending more time with youth who have dropped out.

5. I have too little time for myself.

   Do you see the common theme? Take a look again:

1. When busy, I sacrifice my devotional **time**.

2. The job demands are more than **time** allows.

3. I feel the emotional strain of my work.

4. I regret not spending more **time** with youth who have dropped out.

5. I have too little **time** for myself.

   The greatest threat to youth worker longevity is not our lack of skills or creativity, but our inability to manage the competing, confusing, often chaotic demands on our *time*. Sustainable youth ministers recognize one fact to be true: we'll *never* get it all done. Show me a youth director whose job feels manageable, and there's a good possibility he or she simply doesn't understand the job!

   We discovered the parable we love to use in coaching youth workers in a delightful little book by Brian Tracey called *Eat That Frog*. The parable goes something like this: Every morning, each of us faces a tiny frog on a plate in front of us, a frog that we must, sooner or later, *eat*. Like the slimy little creatures we dissected in biology class, these bite-sized frogs are not the first thing we'd *like* to pop in our mouth. But in the magical world of this parable, the only way we can survive is to eat one little frog a day.

   The frog represents that one task that, if accomplished or ignored, will have the greatest impact on our future or the future of our ministry. Sometimes this task is as simple as making one phone call or setting up one appointment or even reading a chapter of a book that helps equip us to change. Sometimes it's scheduling enough time to draft a strategic plan, setting a time to chip away at a massive, high-priority project or designing a curriculum template that keeps us from the reactive, teach-whatever-I-can-find chaos normal to youth ministry.

The key to becoming a frog-eating champion is to determine the most important task each day before we do anything. If we fail to eat today's frog because we responded instead to the screaming demands before us, the next day we have a bigger problem: two frogs to eat, and one of them is now just a little bit bigger. When a youth worker feels overwhelmed, he or she is typically swimming in a swamp teeming with frogs that have been ignored in favor of secondary priorities.

I was working recently with a young leader drowning in the frogs he'd been ignoring for months (some for years). He desperately wanted to change the trajectory of his life and ministry. So I told him about the frogs. He loved the idea. I asked him to start by making a list of all the tasks he had to do and then to prioritize that list. I asked him to complete the list before doing anything on it.

Easy enough, right? But two weeks later he explained that he simply *didn't have time* to get the list completed—or started. Yet he did have time to email me with random questions multiple times and even to send me a multipage summary of a book he'd just read.

Stuck youth workers stubbornly refuse to slow down enough to find the strategic frogs they must eat if they're to pull out of negative spirals. Many of these youth workers use the time when they could be eating a frog to complain about how much they have to do.

IT'S ABOUT TIME

I've come to believe that the wrong kind of people teach time management. They tend to be the type who alphabetize their spices, who have in their DNA a natural proclivity for order. What people like me (and most youth workers I know) need is an understanding of time management presented by an attention-deficit-disordered, creatively chaotic youth minister.

If I were to write the *ADD Youth Pastor's Guide to Mastering Time,* it would include the following ideas:

Finish before you start. Unless we commit time at the beginning of each day (or the night before) to determine what our first priorities will be, it's unlikely we'll ever get the most important stuff done. Instead of letting other people's agendas decide our own, we must determine, before the day even begins, what we want to have done by the end of the day (and what we will ignore, guilt-free).

Practice the Pareto principle. The Pareto principle (the 80-20 rule) is accurate when it comes to how we invest our time. Approximately 20 percent of our work produces a whopping 80 percent of our results. And the inverse is just as true: 80 percent of the work we do will produce a measly 20 percent of the results.

For a salesman, the time spent selling (not writing reports, organizing the office, attending meetings or responding to messages) is the biggest predictor of success. For the youth worker, time spent with students, developing a volunteer team and doing strategic planning contribute the most to making a youth ministry sustainable. Unfortunately, too many youth pastors seem to find time for everything *but* these three things.

Post-It notes before PalmPilots. I know guys who have all the latest time-management gadgets, but they still can't seem to *do* the most important things first. Don't be fooled. If you are tempted to be gadget happy, make sure you have a simple system in place to attend to your most important tasks of each day. Having a resource that helps us do the less important things more quickly gives the illusion of productivity, but it will only accelerate the directionless churn of your ministry.

Embrace intentional procrastination. Because most of us overestimate how much we can do in a day, intentional procrastination provides a tool for deciding *beforehand* which things will simply not get done today. For example, I choose to intentionally procrastinate on my preparation for speaking. I determine how long I'll need to prepare for a particular message (or wedding or funeral), and I don't start preparing until that much time immediately before the event. These hours tend to be very focused and productive because of the natural rush of adrenaline that comes from knowing that I've *got* to be ready within the next few hours. Those who think they never procrastinate are deluded; we all put things off every day. Intentional procrastination just allows us to put things off *on purpose.*

BALCONY TIME

Far too many of us deal with our time like a five-year-old taking her hundred-pound dog for a walk. Driven by unpredictable, yelping demands, we feel incapable of doing anything to move our ministries in any direction. Our work becomes reduced to a series of erratic steps that takes us nowhere, each step a random replicate of the one before.

The few—the sustainable youth workers—who have been able to let go of the leash have one thing in common: they almost all practice balcony time. No time management tool is nearly as powerful, in our experience, as this one. In balcony time, we step out of the wild, rushing current of *doing* ministry and step into a place where we actually *work on* our ministries.

It wasn't long into my start in youth ministry when I realized I was expected to be an expert at things I knew nothing about. Where, I wondered, was I supposed to have learned how to be an administrator, a manager, a strategist—all essential skills for longevity in ministry? And where could I learn them?

The answer: in the balcony.

Balcony time is the time when we decide what frogs must be eaten first. Whether they're aware of it or not, everyone with leadership responsibility for a youth ministry has all the following responsibilities, which only get attended to properly when there's enough time in the balcony:

- recruiting all leaders for the current ministry as well as all leaders for next year's ministry

- goal setting and strategic planning for the ministry

- getting (and keeping) parents, the senior pastor and the church leaders on your team

- keeping students connected

- developing a plan for discipling every youth in the ministry

- engaging youth in the life of the broader church

- being prepared for crises that youth and families may encounter

- having an intentional curriculum

- making sure youth events are well attended

- reading

- establishing a campus presence

- taking time to care for your own spiritual life

- taking time to rest

Though these items are the very ones most likely to move a youth ministry forward, they are also the ones most likely to be ignored.

Let me be clear. Balcony time is not the same as Sabbath time or devotional time. A Sabbath is a day off from work; balcony time is time *on,* but usually not at the office, where interruptions are likely to come every fifteen minutes. The balcony is the place where we take measures to ensure that our Sabbath time and time with God are protected.

It is in the balcony that we gain the perspective to work *on* our ministries, not just *in* them. In the balcony, we find the leverage to move our ministries forward; it's in the balcony that we move out of a victim mentality and into the mindset of a leader; it's in the balcony that we learn to say no to secondary priorities in order to attend to the most essential ones; it's in the balcony that we *invest* time in our ministries rather than just *spend* time.

Here's how it works: Balcony time begins by carving out a block of at least four hours each week. Sustainable youth workers promise themselves that, during this time, they will not answer the phone, will not respond to emails, will not plan *this* week's programs and will not seek to accomplish anything on the bulging urgent list. Though balcony time is not the place to work on this week's top priorities, it is the place where we determine what those top priorities will be. It's the place where we make the hard decisions about what things we'll intentionally procrastinate about in the coming week.

I like to start my month by identifying the major chunks of time I'll need to do the most important things, beginning with a weekly Sabbath day and three more four-hour blocks each week when I can be available to my family. The next step is to carve out an additional four-hour block each week for balcony time. All my meetings, phone calls and to-do lists get squeezed in around these priorities (Sabbath, family time and balcony time). Of course, the plan never works as neatly as it may look on paper—that's another reason for balcony time. And it's just one more reason we must also learn to become exceptional monkey managers.

WHERE HAVE ALL YOUR MONKEYS GONE?

Every sustainable youth worker I've ever known has, sooner or later, learned the fine art of monkey management. I'm not referring to the skill of corralling that hormonal herd of junior-highers. I'm talking about all the "monkeys on our backs." Simply defined, a monkey is the responsibility to make the next move.

Just walking down the hall at church, a youth pastor is a monkey magnet. In fact, it's not uncommon for us to walk out of church on any given Sunday carrying twenty or so new monkeys. The monkeys climb on our backs through innocent comments like these (just for effect, you're welcome to hum the flying-monkey music from *The Wizard of Oz* as you read):

- "My son doesn't feel connected to the youth group."

- "I've got a soccer game on Saturday."

- "Will you pray for me this week?"

- "Jim broke his collarbone and could really use a call."

- "I'd like to give the youth ministry ten thousand dollars."

- "Our family is thinking about leaving the church."

Youth workers most prone to being overwhelmed by flying monkeys are those who walk down the halls of the church saying things like, "I'll call you this week about that." They end phone conversations with "Let me think about it and get back to you on that later this week." They tend to end meetings having discussed an issue to death, but without knowing who will deal with all the monkeys.

Unless managed properly, screaming monkeys *will* overwhelm us and keep us from leading our ministries forward. After thirty years in the jungle of monkey management, I've observed a few principles about the behavior of these monkeys, patterns that every monkey management master needs to know:

- *Monkeys always climb.* Monkeys tend to climb up an organizational chart. If I haven't managed a monkey well, I can be sure that it won't be long before that monkey will be dancing on my boss's desk (leaving disgusting little monkey droppings).

- *Mismanaged monkeys multiply.* When my senior pastor gets a call from a parent who says, "I talked to our youth director about it, but *nothing* has happened," I suddenly have two monkeys—the original monkey from the parent and the new monkey of convincing my senior pastor that I'm not an irresponsible idiot.

- *A monkey is soon forgotten.* The dullest pencil is better than the sharpest memory. When I take on a monkey, I have to write it down. A monkey left alone only gets wilder.

- *Never accept a monkey on the run.* When someone tries to hand me a monkey as I'm rushing somewhere, I simply ask if that person could put a note on my desk or leave me a message. Whenever possible, I always like to leave the person most concerned about the monkey with the responsibility to take the next step.

- *Hidden monkeys stagnate ministries.* So many of our meetings accomplish so little because, when the meeting is over, monkeys are left hiding under the table. If I've talked about an issue for ten minutes with six people, and no one leaves with a monkey (that is, the responsibility to *do* something), we've just wasted an hour.

- *A monkey sent is not necessarily a monkey received.* We recently sent a proposal to a senior pastor who had requested it for a meeting he was having ten days later. Although we emailed him the proposal three days after his request, it didn't make it through the spam filter at his church. Our follow-up calls two weeks later received an icy reception. We had *assumed* that because we sent the message, it actually made it. It was our responsibility, our monkey, to make sure our message was received—and we dropped it.

- *Screaming monkeys want all of our attention.* Screaming monkeys— urgent calls that must be returned, the youth group kid who is hospitalized, the unexpected expectations of other staff members, parents and kids—are a natural part of youth ministry. But coddling screaming monkeys seldom moves a ministry forward and often distracts us from the strategic work we have to do. Wise monkey managers give the screaming monkeys their due, but they never sacrifice the things that matter most on the altar of the things that scream the loudest.

- *It's hard to manage monkeys when we're hugging them.* Far too many youth directors are monkey collectors, rather than monkey managers. They take charge by hording responsibility, by keeping responsibility away from key volunteers and other staff people. In doing so, they become the biggest bottleneck to the ministry's forward progress. The only way all our monkeys get managed is if we put together a monkey management team and make it one of our first priorities to ensure that every ministry monkey has a manager.

- *A monkey given to a group is a monkey given to no one.* Ask some senior pastors who's responsible for a certain aspect of their church's ministry, and they will give you the name of a committee. But committees can't be responsible; only individuals can. As the old cliché goes, "When everyone is responsible, no one is responsible." And when no one is responsible, ultimately the pastor becomes responsible. It's okay for the committee to own the responsibility for a ministry *area*, but responsibility to initiate the next step must be owned by an individual.

- *Monkeys are managed best when they're near the ground.* Because we know that monkeys tend to climb up the organizational chart (see the first monkey management principle on this list), the greatest hope is to push the monkeys as far "down" the organization as possible. Those at the bottom of the organizational chart often are the most motivated to manage their monkeys. For example, if a senior pastor (at the top of the organizational chart) tells his staff he'll bring a report to the next meeting and then fails to deliver, he has simply procrastinated. But if that pastor tells his youth pastor to bring the report, and he or she doesn't do it, the youth pastor has just been insubordinate. The same is true at some level with volunteers. If a volunteer has just one assignment (bringing cookies to the party, for example), that person is more likely to get it done than the youth worker, who has to remember fifty other things for the event.

- *Monkeys weren't made for badminton.* We've met a few passive-aggressive youth workers who love to play badminton with monkeys. They slam at monkeys, saying things like, "Don't try to put that monkey on me!" "That's not my monkey!" "Don't ask me; you're the expert." Sustainable youth workers thrive on taking responsibility by solving problems, not avoiding them.

- *Beware of sticky monkeys.* If someone wants to start a Boy Scout troop at the church, and the youth worker shows up to the organizational meeting, he or she should be prepared for everyone to look to him or her to lead it. If someone comes to a youth worker with a new ministry idea, unless the youth worker makes it clear otherwise, when the idea-bringer gets tired of the ministry, he or she will look to that youth staff person to keep it alive.

SHOWING UP FOR PRACTICE

Every youth ministry faces chronic challenges that resist the normal solutions of prayer, planning and persistence. Whether a church is attempting to turn around a stalled youth ministry or moving its thriving youth ministry off a plateau, those churches require the kind of single-minded, synergistic energy that only comes from a team that regularly "practices" together. And there is only one word for those practices, a word distasteful to most youth workers: *meetings.*

If we're going to navigate around brick walls, we need more than a patchwork collection of ideas implemented in unpredictable episodes by passionate individuals. We need the power of a team pulling together in a unified, crystal-clear direction. Getting a team pulling in the same direction requires that the members regularly "show up for practice."

Unfortunately, meetings led by creative, relational youth workers tend to swirl and churn, addressing dozens of issues with the same level of time and energy, often leaving the most important topics to the point in the meeting when "time is up." These meetings offer an illusion of movement but never actually move ministries forward, because they fall victim to classic meeting mistakes:

> You need a driver's license to operate a car but no qualifications to call a meeting, which means any fool can do so. You're bound to suffer folly in meetings—especially church meetings, which have been known to last through several presidential administrations.
>
> MIKE WOODRUFF

- a loose, free-flowing, unwritten agenda

- a leader who expresses his or her opinion early in the meeting

- an unspoken rule that anyone who questions an idea will be labeled as mean-spirited and hypercritical

- a tradition of having everyone at the table report on his or her areas of responsibility, even if it means reporting what everyone in the group already knows

One of the reasons so many youth ministries—and so many churches, for that matter—are chronically stuck is that they fail to access the power of good meetings.

In his marvelous book-length parable, *Death by Meeting,* Patrick Lencioni suggests that thriving organizations need three distinctly different kinds of meetings:

1. Daily stand-up meetings at the beginning of each day (five minutes)—standing up to ensure brevity, daily to ensure accountability. Nothing affected the productivity of our summer interns like having daily stand-up meetings to make sure each intern had clarity about his or her number-one priority for the day.

> **The single biggest structural problem facing leaders of meetings is the tendency to throw every type of issue that needs to be discussed into the same meeting, like a bad stew with too many random ingredients.**
>
> PATRICK LENCIONI

2. Weekly tactical meetings (an hour to an hour and a half). These meetings keep the team focused on the immediate concerns, the tasks and responsibilities that require the sharing of information and coordination of effort. In youth ministry, it's normal to talk about scheduling, volunteer recruitment and support, attendance, and kids and families in need of immediate attention.

3. Monthly or quarterly strategic meetings (two to eight hours).

- For churches with more than one youth staff person, these meetings tend to be longer (typically four to eight hours) and involve taking time away as a team for soul-tending, dealing with long-term strategic issues, launching new initiatives, creating strategies for moving together over the most critical obstacle facing the ministry.

- For churches with only one staff person, these meetings are shorter (one to two-and-a-half hours) and involve a focused cadre of leaders who work together on a specific speed bump that's hindering the ministry.

Also, I like to pull my team away for an annual retreat to do long-term visioning and scheduling, in addition to growing in our love for each other and for Christ together. At these meetings away, we take time to address chronic challenges, including the following:

- getting kids to go to worship

- growing the group beyond a plateau

- putting a shepherding program in place that ensures that every youth is known and pursued by an adult in the church

- motivating kids to engage in mission

These challenges will not be met without the power of a team moving in the same direction—praying, dreaming, trying, failing, evaluating, trying again, praying some more.

WANTED: THIRD-PIG YOUTH WORKERS

When I read *The Three Little Pigs*, I can't help but see the first two pigs as metaphors for traditional youth ministry. They built their houses fast, considering the deliberate work of the third pig just a little obsessive for their tastes. And, quite frankly, the first two pigs achieved visible results much faster than their brick-laying brother.

But when the wolf showed up with his huffing and puffing, the little pigs were left with nothing stronger than their brash confidence and bold conviction: "I won't let you in! Not by the hair of my chinny chin chin!" But words are cheap when no structure is in place to back those words up.

Normal, everyday, garden-variety youth workers throw the structure of their ministries together quickly and then scurry around, mired in their own complaints about their senior pastors and elders, bemoaning the hopeless state of youth ministry around the world.

Sustainable youth workers spend their time eating frogs, climbing balconies and actually enjoying the wild and woolly monkey dance that is always a part of youth ministry. Third-pig youth ministers build sustainable youth ministries one brick at a time—ministries that won't be blown in.

10

ARCHITECTING THE CONSTELLATION

From Camp Counselor to Sustainable Leader

*What youth need more than gung-ho adults are Godbearing adults,
people whose own yes to God has transformed them into messengers
of the gospel.*

KENDA DEAN AND RON FOSTER

*Reams of material are written and taught with an approach to reaching
an end by effortless means—and more will be written. Advertising
messages continually promote methods of achieving end results with
little or no effort. And this material and these messages are so effective
that in many cases people will work harder to avoid the extra effort
than actually applying the extra effort that will produce the originally
desired outcome.*

S. L. PARKER

I started a recent seminar with a simple brainstorming statement: The
biggest problem with volunteers is . . .

The first person shouted, "What volunteers?!" And with a wave of
laughter, the brainstorm was launched. Someone said, "They stay in the
back of the room and don't talk to kids." Another gave just the opposite

response: "They try to take over." A third shouted, "It's impossible to fire them!" As each answer was written on the board, heads nodded.

Every now and then, people ask us, "With all the different kinds of churches you work with, do you see patterns that show up in every church youth ministry?" The answer is an unequivocal yes. Once the youth staff is in place, there's no challenge youth ministries face more consistently than fielding a well-equipped, well-coordinated team of volunteers.

Unfortunately, most churches perfectly design their youth ministries to guarantee volunteer problems. Here's how: they hire camp counselors to lead their youth ministry instead of ministry leaders.

Now, there's nothing wrong with having a "camp counselor" working with youth. In fact, having people who see their primary role as building relationships with kids is crucial to every youth ministry. But we have a name for folks who play that role, a name that just might surprise you: *volunteers.*

WHY VOLUNTEERS MATTER

Remember our pyramid from chapter five:

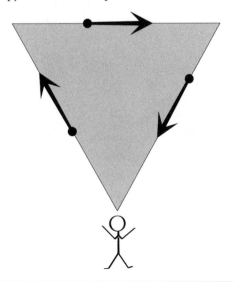

Figure 8.

Youth ministry is the *church's* ministry, not just that of specialists who can "relate" to young people. The mandate to *be there* for young people belongs to the Christian *community*, not to any individual or group of individuals.

KENDA DEAN

The only way to turn this pyramid upside down is through the development of a team of volunteer leaders. But the unanticipated consequence of the elevation of the "profession" of youth ministry has been to push the work of volunteers to the sidelines. Too many volunteer leaders see themselves as second-class assistants to the *real* ministers doing the work. If volunteers (what some call "unpaid staff") are to be empowered to serve, there must be someone charged with the responsibility of cultivating these leaders.

Sadly, the typical professional in youth ministry continues to see his or her primary job as "relating to students," one student at a time, something like figure 9.

Figure 9.

The camp counselor role works just fine, as long as the number of youth involved in the program stays low. But if the ministry grows, the picture begins to look more like figure 10.

Figure 10.

The result of growing a youth ministry through a camp counselor is the implosion of the youth ministry (and often the youth minister).

But what would happen if professional youth workers took the radical step of seeing their relationship with students as *secondary*? What would happen if, instead, youth workers recognized that their primary work was ensuring that each student in the ministry had multiple godly adults pouring into his or her life? What would happen if we reconfigured youth ministry in such a way that the paid youth worker was primarily the *architect of a constellation of relationships?* It might look more like figure 11.

Figure 11.

Notice the shift at the center of the last two diagrams. In this last design, the teenager is no longer a dangling appendage, no longer dependent on the faithfulness, longevity or availability of a single member of the body of Christ. Rather, that young person is at the center of a web, a convergent community connected not only to him or her but also to each other.

Could it be that one of the reasons teenagers in our culture have such a hard time developing an integrated identity is that they are surrounded with dis-integrating relationships? Could it be that fragmented relationships with people who know nothing of each other actually pull teenagers away from an integrating center, leaving them with a patch-work identity developed as a coping mechanism for surviving the root-lessness of their world?

This letter from a teenage girl to her small-group leader (a volunteer) captures some of the power that a durable adult can have in a student's life:

> This was the first year that I ever felt included. . . . I knew that someone really did love me. . . . You made the insecure ones feel secure, making the excluded ones included. You loved me, spent time with me, and wanted to see me know God more. No one has ever done that for me before.

But behind this story is another story: this connection would never have happened unless the leader of the ministry (typically the paid staff person behind the unpaid staff person) had taken time away from "being with kids" to train and to transfer ministry responsibility and authority to this volunteer leader.

Everybody loves the idea of having more volunteers. We all understand *why*. But it is the *how* that's the problem. After experimenting with a wide variety of methods for building volunteer teams in churches with all kinds of internal and external obstacles, we've identified three essential steps for building a thriving volunteer youth ministry team (and thus, a thriving youth ministry): recruitment, developing a team and delegating.

RECRUITMENT: THE FIRST STEP IS THE HARDEST

The study behind the book *Youth Ministry That Transforms* revealed that less than a third of professional youth workers experience regular success in recruiting volunteers. Less than a third! Our experience with youth workers bears this statistic out.

Quite accidentally, we stumbled onto the biggest obstacle in recruiting volunteer leaders. After working with church after church that just couldn't seem to get traction in recruiting volunteers, we started asking youth workers, "How many hours have you spent in the previous week actually recruiting volunteers?" Almost invariably, it was less than an hour (most often, it was exactly zero).

To get a youth worker off the dime, we recommend that he or she make five recruiting calls in the coming week. Since at this point we're not expecting a definite yes or no, we call these "cultivating calls" rather than recruiting calls. The assignment is not to recruit, but simply to make the first call (even if that is simply leaving a message). This process can take anywhere from ten to thirty minutes.

Before we end our conversation with the youth worker, we agree on the names of people he or she will call for what volunteer positions and agree to an accountability check the next week.

But when we check in a week later, the youth worker who "desperately" wants more volunteers has often not made a single call. *Something* has come up—an unusually busy ministry month, a student in crisis, a dog who ate the list.

We're talking about an assignment that could have been completed in less than thirty minutes, maybe in as little as ten. But the average youth worker has extraordinary difficulty finding those ten minutes.

Here's why: Recruiting is hard.

Few of us like to ask people to do things for us. Most of us would rather just do it ourselves than go through the discomfort of making calls. As a result, many youth workers step into the fall (when the season opens) unable to field a complete team and complaining about being overwhelmed.

This pattern perpetuates the myth that "no one in our church ever volunteers." Frantically cobbling together a group of volunteers who fill slots every other week or so reinforces the perception that they're only helpers in someone else's ministry. When we see a youth ministry with rotating helpers, we can be sure that there is dry rot in the foundation.

Sadly, most volunteer recruitment comes in the form of blanket solicitations to large groups. The assumption, of course, is that such an approach will save the recruiter time. But in the long run, blanket appeals always wind up taking *more* time, for very obvious reasons:

- Blanket appeals often attract volunteers who would simply not be appropriate to work with teenagers (I refer to blanket bulletin appeals as "pedophile invitations"). Getting the wrong person to stop being involved takes a lot more time than never having him or her involved in the first place.

- The kind of initiative-taking leaders we're looking for seldom flock to blanket announcements. They need to be recruited personally, one at a time. They'll need to be contacted anyway, so blanket appeals only multiply the amount of time required.

- A flurry of public announcements about the *desperate need* in the youth ministry perpetuates a climate of desperation, which almost always results in a flurry of unsolicited advice-giving from well-meaning church members and senior pastors who assume they need to help the youth worker to fix his or her problem.

But hidden beneath all the reasons recruiting doesn't work, there's good news: when those responsible for a youth ministry actually invest the appropriate amount of time in the recruitment process, at the right time, we can almost guarantee success.

We've seen lots of variations, shortcuts and "brilliant" ideas for recruiting volunteers (for example, some suggest that you have the kids recruit for you, or threaten to cancel a program if you don't have enough volunteers), but none of those work nearly as well as *working* a very clear process. Remember, we're investing, not gambling on great ideas.

In this chapter, I want to offer the keystone steps of any effective recruiting process. Churches that stick to these fundamentals *will* almost always have the number of volunteers they want.

WORKING THE RECRUITMENT PROCESS

If you're expecting a secret, new-and-improved way of recruiting volunteers, you might be disappointed with what you're about to read.

Churches who buy into the latest-and-greatest, cutting-edge approaches to recruiting typically find themselves with limited results. Here's the very straightforward process that, when worked, actually works:

1. Start early. We like to suggest that churches open their recruiting season for the coming year at least six months before the potential leaders are to begin serving. This principle means that most youth ministries need to begin their major recruiting push in February.

When we make these recommendations, people smile, as if to say, "That will never work around here. People don't commit that far in advance." But we've discovered that the very people we *want* to serve as leaders actually do think this way. These are the kind of people who take their commitments seriously enough that they know *today* whether they'll be the chairperson for the PTA or on the board of the United Way or Rotary six months from now. The earlier you ask, the more weight you give to the role you're asking the potential volunteer to play.

2. Identify your needs. Strangely enough, most youth ministers never sit down to discover how many volunteers they actually need to sustain their ministry for the coming year. Most imagine that they're somehow *beyond* having to write down a list of needs; they simply assume they can keep it in their head (reason number one for why recruiting seldom makes it to the top of their to-do lists).

Figuring out the number of volunteers needed begins by taking out a pen and paper (or sitting down at a computer) and listing all the volunteers who will be required for the coming year, such as

- Sunday school teachers

- Sunday school helpers

- youth group leaders

- small group leaders

- prayer partners/shepherds

- retreat leaders

- major-event coordinators

- youth committee members

We typically recommend a ratio of one adult for every five youth that the church hopes to see active in the ministry. In other words, a church with a dream of having fifty active students weekly should have ten volunteers engaged in hands-on leadership on a weekly basis. This number typically doesn't include the dozens of other volunteers who will work behind the scenes, like committee members and event coordinators.

A quick word of explanation about major-event coordinators: If you have ever lived in a midsize to large city, you've probably heard of an organization called Junior League, made up of women who work together to pull off grand events that raise money for their favorite charities. I watched from a distance as Junior League in Nashville put on events, and I compared it to the way I was working. Here's what I discovered:

- They raise tens (sometimes hundreds) of thousands of dollars with their events.

- These events are run almost entirely by volunteers, and they're much more intricate and involved than any event our youth ministry has ever tried to pull off.

- I was spending inordinate amounts of time organizing events (everything from arranging for food to reserving transportation to finding photographers). And I'm not particularly good at organizing events.

- I had well over a hundred women in my church who had experience serving in organizations like the Junior League.

- Many of these women's kids had forbidden them from being youth leaders or Sunday school teachers.

- Instead of asking these mothers to do load-bearing work in the ministry, I was asking them to bring half a dozen cookies once a year to an event, when they would have been doing a much better job organizing than I was or ever could.

It's always fun to discover a new way to spell *stupid* using the letters of my own name.

A fascinating thing happened when I started allowing highly organized people to organize our events: they got organized. The capacity of our ministry expanded dramatically, because I was freed to do the things only I could do, like recruiting and equipping volunteers.

3. Develop your pool. The next step is to develop a pool of potential recruits. Most youth ministries recruit "off the cuff." They discover a need (usually an urgent one), and they do what comes naturally—they go after the best person they can find for that position. Sounds logical, doesn't it?

The danger of this approach is that you may be asking an A player to do a job that a C player could do just as well—or better. For example, when you've got to have someone make the arrangements for the cookout, your mind immediately turns to Jan. Jan is an uber-volunteer; she can do just about anything. She's clearly the best pick for this job (and just about any other job you might need her to do). You call Jan, and she's happy to say yes.

Two weeks later, you need someone to handle all the logistics for the silent auction, the extraordinarily complicated fundraiser that should bring in 90 percent of the money needed for the upcoming mission trip. You immediately think of Jan, but her youth ministry volunteer plate is now filled with the less-strategic job of managing the cookout.

Strategic recruitment means waiting to make the first recruiting call until you've developed a master list of potential volunteers. We suggest going through your entire church directory and writing down every name of every person who might be a potential volunteer, and putting those names in one of three categories:

1. working directly with students

2. working behind the scenes (like a major-event coordinator)

3. working either with students or behind the scenes

The general rule is to develop a list three times longer than the number of volunteers you actually need.

Once that list is developed, label each name on the list. You can use any system you like, but I like the baseball approach:

- Babe Ruths (the *A*s)—those players you believe would "knock it out of the park" if they took on a position in the youth ministry

- utility infielders (the *B*s)—those players who would do a fine job

- pinch hitters (the *C*s)—the potential volunteers who would "do in a pinch"

This is not the time for us to make a decision *for* our potential volunteers. In other words, this is not the time to say, "She would never do it." At this point, we're simply developing the list of people we believe have the gifts for this kind of ministry, even if we don't believe they have the time right now.

4. Select a draft pick for every position. Once you have the two lists in front of you (the list of needs for your ministry and the list of potential leaders), place a name next to every position. Add phone numbers, and use this document as the master recruiting list. I always like to start with the "reach recruits," those superstars (like the senior pastor) who I think have little chance of saying yes. If they say no, I've lost nothing. But I'm surprised how often someone I'm sure won't be available says yes.

5. Start smiling and dialing. The traditional way of recruiting requires waiting until you think someone will be at home before making calls. This approach is problematic for a number of reasons:

- It assumes people will be more likely to say yes because of your powers of persuasion. The opposite is usually true: if people feel forced into an answer, they will tend to say no.

- It provides an excuse for not making calls immediately. "Just the right time to call" seldom comes, leaving the procrastinating recruiter a month further down the road with nothing to show for it.

- It avoids the most polite ways of communicating the opportunity to serve as a potential leader. Leaving a message by email or voicemail allows your prospect to consider and pray through the opportunity without feeling pressure to respond immediately.

When you call, ask for what you really want. Avoid making the position too easy. Our senior consultant Jeff Dunn-Rankin has helped me imagine how Jesus might recruit if he used the same methods that many of us use in youth ministry. Jeff imagines that the revised biblical text might go something like this:

> And verily Jesus saw Peter, busy with his day job, and said reluctantly unto him, "Listen, man, I need you to do me a favor. Nobody's responded to my note in the bulletin, and I can't get anybody to help us out on this thing I'm putting together. I don't know what happened to commitment, but hey, whatever. I just need you to spend some time with me once a month. You and Nathanael and Judas could do it on a rotating basis. Look, I know you're busy, but if you do this I'll definitely owe you one. If not, we're canceling the Last Supper."

6. *When two-thirds of your potential leaders turn you down, return to step four and repeat the process.* The secret is not in the creativity of the process; it is in persistently *working* the process. Committing the time and fighting the inertia of call resistance are key aspects of a recruiting program that short-term, camp-counselor youth workers avoid. Starting the recruiting process six months in advance provides enough margin for repeating the process over and over until you have a full team to field, before the insanity of summer schedules arrives.

DEVELOPING THE VOLUNTEER TEAM:
STEWARDING A COMMUNITY OF DREAMERS

Once a team is in place for the year, it's time to ensure that systems are in place to help those leaders discover their unique calls to ministry while at the same time moving toward a single, clearly articulated vision. I love Erwin McManus's winsome picture of our role in working with volunteers. He calls us "stewards of a community of dreamers."

In their landmark study of professional youth workers, Merton Strommen, Dave Rahn and Karen Jones discovered that 70 percent of youth pastors considered "developing volunteers" to be either "very important" or "extremely important." But less than 25 percent of that same group said they'd been able to develop volunteers effectively, and half reported little or no success at all.

There are few places where the Second Law of Thermodynamics ("things tend toward a state of disorder") is more apparent than in the development of volunteers. We can be certain that if we don't have systems in place to intentionally empower, train and encourage our volunteers, they *will not* fulfill the responsibilities the ministry requires of them.

> Most organizations are a puzzle put together in a darkened room. Each piece is clumsily squeezed into place and then the edges are ground down so that they feel well positioned. But pull up the shades, let a little light into the room, and we can see the truth. Eight out of ten pieces are in the wrong place.
>
> MARCUS BUCKINGHAM AND DONALD CLIFTON

The simple (but not easy) principle of investment holds true here as well. Ministries that invest time troubleshooting, clarifying and connecting their volunteers build effective teams. Those who leave volunteer training to chance wind up with a dream team of amazingly gifted leaders who never seem to get enough traction to move their ministries forward.

What do leaders of highly effective ministry teams do differently?

They communicate. I have a friend who was asked by a ministry organization to "help" lead a mission trip to Iowa for a small group of teenagers. Just days before the trip, he learned that he would be the trip's only adult. The trip, filled with one unpleasant surprise after another, left him with the conviction that he would never work with teenagers again.

> Getting good players, that's the easy part. Getting them to play together, that's the hard part.
>
> CASEY STENGEL

Every volunteer longs for clarity. But too often we give only fuzzy expectations—no job description, no behavioral covenant, no accountability structure—and then wonder why our volunteers don't last.

One youth worker I know, when encouraged to spend more time supporting his volunteers, said that if the volunteers didn't feel comfortable "just hanging out with kids," he didn't need them. You can imagine how eager his new recruits were to return to youth group after being ignored by the person they thought would give them direction.

Youth ministry can be filled with frustration and deep discouragement, especially for inexperienced volunteers. Without persistent troubleshooting and intentional support, most youth ministry volunteers simply don't continue. Not all volunteers need the same thing: some need encouragement, others need coaching and still others need help transitioning, as soon as possible, to another ministry. Regular communication takes time, the kind of time a camp-counselor youth worker will not spend.

They celebrate. In our church, one of the best times to recruit volunteers is at the end of the senior banquet. After an extended evening that includes teenagers speaking their hearts to those who have led them over the previous six years, volunteers leave with little doubt that their sacrificial commitment has "changed the world," at least for a few kids. Few things are more motivating than someone hearing his or her name mentioned as a young person tells about the transformation God has worked in his or her life.

Youth ministries with effective volunteer teams find ways to give affirmation and encouragement all year long. For instance,

- the church that gives its youth leaders Starbucks cards periodically, thanking them for their countless hours invested in kids

- the youth pastor who invites every volunteer or volunteer couple to his or her home for dinner at least once a year, just to say thanks

- the senior pastor who mentions in sermons the selfless contribution of the adults in the church who work with students

They do ministry out of community. I'm convinced that one reason youth ministries fail to build a magnetic community among their teenagers is because the adults who work with them have few, if any, connections *with each other.* It's mighty hard to cultivate a sense of family among our kids if that same sense isn't present among the adults.

I'm also convinced that one of the reasons Young Life volunteers do such an extraordinary job of building relationships with students outside the context of Young Life meetings is because those leaders generally meet together *every week.* The actual content of those meetings is less important than the practice of simply logging the quantity time necessary for a group of individuals to function like the body of Christ.

They build the expectation of long-term continuation. People laugh when I tell them that, at our church, we ask our youth ministry volunteers to stay involved for six years. My experience is that asking people to work with teenagers for less than that robs them of the sweetest part of doing youth ministry: watching the kids who once wore them out grow into godly men and women.

Mike Nappa discovered in his study *What I Wish My Youth Leader Knew About Youth Ministry* that, with some variation by grade, between 33 percent and 42 percent of youth group students said that their volunteer leaders had a great deal of influence on their involvement in youth group. But that number jumps significantly for the seniors, 51 percent of whom describe their volunteer leaders' role as "having a great deal of influence." I don't think it's too much of an interpretive leap to assume that these volunteer leaders were not newly introduced during the senior year. More likely, they were reaping the fruit of long, durable relationships built over a span of years, not weeks.

DELEGATING: THE POWER OF AN APPRENTICING CULTURE

Calvin and Hobbes are speeding down the hill in the little red wagon. Calvin says to his tiger friend, "I thrive on change!"

Hobbes responds skeptically, "You? You threw a fit this morning because your mom put less jelly on your toast than yesterday."

Calvin revises his statement, "I thrive on making other people change."

Most people see delegation as getting other people to do the work they don't want to do themselves. But abdication and abandonment are not the same as delegation.

In an abandonment culture, volunteers learn never to volunteer for anything, never to suggest an idea, because if they do, they "get stuck with it for life." In an apprenticing culture, volunteers have all the support they need every step of the way, from the one-on-one orientation meeting to the final victory dance—and all the troubleshooting in between.

Most youth workers I know despise meetings. But for our ministries to be consistent, the unpredictable people who serve in our ministries need a predictable structure. When we assume that our volunteers will naturally do what we expect them to do, we delude ourselves. They will do only one thing predictably: be unpredictable.

Rosabeth Moss Kanter discovered in her fascinating study of winning streaks and losing streaks in business that

> the losing companies are twice as likely as the winning companies to have reduced the number of management meetings in the preceding two years. At the very time when communication is most needed, losers are more likely to stop talking. . . . Losers, compared with winners, are nearly four times as likely to keep information in the hands of a small group that operates in secrecy behind closed doors, shutting everyone else out.

In "winning" organizations, information flows freely; in "losing" organizations, a select few hold the information. Meetings are nowhere more important than in the delegation of responsibility to key volunteers. Three kinds of meetings are pivotal to developing this apprenticeship culture: orientation, check-in and celebration.

1. *The orientation.* At this meeting, the ministry leader and the volunteer talk through the specific job description, the youth leader covenant, the overall mission of the youth ministry, and the unique scope

and sequence of the work to be done. If we hope to give our volunteers load-bearing responsibility—the only kind that's truly satisfying for a volunteer—this is essential.

During this orientation meeting, the leader might learn the specifics of building relationships with students, the general concept he or she agreed to initially. For example, a weekly volunteer might learn that he or she is responsible to

- participate weekly in an assigned ministry setting (Sunday school, youth group or small-group Bible study)

- spend thirty minutes a week being in touch with his or her assigned students (for example, one week by phone, the next by email, the next by letter, the next by attending a student's game or going out for coffee)

- attend regular youth leader meetings

2. The periodic check-in. Why does Barry Bonds have a batting coach? Why does Tiger Woods have a swing coach? Because fundamentals break down, even if you're the best in the league. Without a periodic check-in, we abandon our volunteers to their own memories, and we prevent them from part of the experience they thought they would get when they said yes: interacting with *us*.

No matter how much of a self-starter the volunteer is, he or she will need regular follow-up from you. We may imagine that the more competent the volunteer, the less we'll need to check in with him or her. Surprisingly, the opposite is true. When we fail to give strong leaders clear direction, we give them permission to take the project in any direction they want, regardless of whether or not that direction fits with the mission and values of our ministry. Taking time for a five-minute check-in can save countless hours and maximize the chances of our best volunteers being willing to serve again.

3. The celebration. Too many volunteers complete their term of sacrificial service and no one says a word. Whether the celebration takes the form of a ten-minute post-event "afterglow" with all the key players celebrating together or a thank-you dinner, effective volunteer teams always take time to celebrate.

When these volunteer development processes are clearly in place, momentum begins to take over. For the past ten years or so, our church has sponsored an annual parenting seminar, followed by a youth workers seminar by a nationally known youth leader. At first, our results were disappointing at best. But this past year, we experienced the power of momentum in full effect.

When we met with Justin and Maureen Milam, our incredible volunteer chairpeople, three or four months before the event, we outlined the responsibilities, built in a few systems for periodic check-ins and got out of the way. Because they had served as lead volunteers before, they knew exactly what they were getting into, and they handled this responsibility with even greater effectiveness than in previous roles. And each year they got better, we all got better.

FIFTY THOUSAND COACHES

In the middle of the delightful movie *Akeelah and the Bee,* Akeelah, a gifted young girl from an inner-city school, has hit a brick wall: the master spelling coach who was to be her ticket to winning the national spelling bee has resigned.

Akeelah's mother tries to comfort her, telling the story of her own attempt at college and how her fear of failure led her to drop out. As they sit on the couch, Akeelah's mom herself begins to coach Akeelah on her spelling words. Finally, mother challenges daughter triumphantly, "I'll bet there are fifty thousand coaches out there."

A youth worker's job is to help students access their own collection of fifty thousand coaches, not to be a solo coaching superstar. Someone described a manager as the person who takes care of the visitors so that everyone else can get their work done. It's not a bad description for a sustainable youth minister: taking care of all the distractions, so that God's people can do the work God has called them to do.

11

THE MAGNET EFFECT

Making Friendship Contagious

When people are overwhelmed with information and develop immunity to traditional forms of communication, they turn instead for advice and information to the people in their lives whom they respect, admire, and trust.

MALCOLM GLADWELL

Suppose one of you has a hundred sheep and loses one of them. Does he not leave the ninety-nine in the open country and go after the lost sheep until he finds it?

JESUS, IN LUKE 15:4

Daniel Goleman claims that the high school dropout rate of children who are rejected by their peers is between two and eight times greater than that of children who are accepted.

DONALD MILLER

Typically, churches have viewed adolescents as objects of mission, not as agents of mission.

KENDA DEAN

Catie was the third generation in her family to grow up in our church. Her parents helped to launch a young-adult Sunday school class. Her grandfather was an elder. We always called her dad first when we had a question about technology. My daughter babysat for Catie and her brother as they were growing up. Catie was well liked and popular at school, a beautiful young woman with a bubbly, magnetic personality.

But after her eighth-grade year, neither she nor her parents were around church much. And so I called. The answer I heard gave me a sick feeling in the pit of my stomach. After a good bit of probing and prodding, Catie summed up for her mom the reason she never wanted to come back to our group: "I'll never be cool enough to fit in there."

How was that possible? So many of the adult leaders were crazy about Catie. She was dependable, comfortable in her own skin, mature beyond her years. We loved having Catie around.

But, because she went to a school attended by few of our youth group members, she was often left out of conversations. And because most middle-schoolers obsessively focus on making *themselves* feel comfortable, none of her peers were taking initiative to make "the outsider" (the one we all assumed was the insider) feel at home and comfortable.

Remember—you'll be at church.

People will be judging you.

DESPERATE HOUSEWIVES

So Catie and her family, whom we had pegged as those most likely to be at the heart of our ministry, left our church. Though it was the last thing they wanted to do, her parents moved their membership to a church where they knew Catie would thrive. She is now deeply involved in a marvelous youth ministry down the street from us, a place where she immediately felt welcome and never once had to wonder if she was "cool enough" to belong.

THE COOL CHURCH

Because of my strong emphasis on family-based youth ministry over the past fifteen years or so, I've argued passionately that what kids need most is not just a group of Christian peers but also droves of durable,

Christian adults. But I'm starting to broaden my appreciation for the unique role the youth themselves can play.

No one brought this principle home to me as clearly as Rick Lawrence did in *Group Magazine*'s fascinating study of ten thousand youth group kids. They asked students, "If you were choosing a church, how important would the following things be?" Check out the first two responses, both of which ranked way above all the others (numbers represent the percentage of kids who rated this item as "very important"):

1. a welcoming environment where I can be myself—73 percent

2. quality relationships with teenagers—70 percent

When *kids* are thinking about the church they might want to be a part of, they're not—at least not initially—thinking about the adult leaders. They're asking, "Are these the kind of people I would like to be friends with?" Interestingly, the third-highest response, coming in at 59 percent, was "a senior pastor who understands and loves teenagers." Coming in near the bottom of the list was "quality relationships with adults" (only 36 percent). And bringing up the rear with only 21 percent was "a fast-paced, high-tech, entertaining ministry approach."

The article that reported this study, incidentally, was called "The Cool Church." If we were to borrow Catie's language, this would not be a church that looks cool to everyone who comes, but rather a church in which "*I feel* cool enough" to belong.

Please understand. Youth not ranking "relationships with adults" high on the list does not minimize the profound role adults play. Long-term, sustainable faith is most deeply influenced by the adults that surround our kids, not just their peers. But as we look at what causes kids to stay in groups, peers play a central role, a role that most adults simply can't play.

As I look back on my experience as the new kid at church, the results of this study ring true. At eleven years old, I moved to Texas with my mom, and we quickly found Central Presbyterian Church in downtown Waco. The service was predictable enough, the adults were nice enough, but when it came time for "fellowship hour," I wanted to throw up.

As my mother "fellowshiped" with all the other fellowshipers, I was left to stand in my prepubescent body by the ten-cent Coke machine. Kids of all ages with dimes in hand walked past me to the Coke machine, gathered their bargain prize and walked away. Though a few gave a polite hello, most were just as uncomfortable having a new kid around as I was standing there.

It wasn't until Thereasa, an angelic tenth-grader, introduced herself to me that my terror started to thaw, and I began to think there might be a chance I would find a place. Every time she invited me to sit next to her, it was an affirmation that I had a place, that I really was starting to belong.

Thereasa did what the adults in the group couldn't have done. She made me feel like part of the group. It's not that adults were insignificant (they became more important as time went on), but adults could not be the sticky paper that kept me connected to the church. Friends had to be.

Once I began to grasp the power of these principles a few years ago, our youth ministry team decided we wanted to make our group the safest, most welcoming place in the city for teenagers, a place where no one could ever walk away saying "I could never be cool enough" to fit in there.

PLANTING THE SEEDS OF A FRIENDSHIP EPIDEMIC

Though Catie, Rick and Thereasa helped me to understand the importance of building a friendship culture in youth ministry, it was my friend Jeanne Mayo who began to teach me how to make it happen. Around the time that her book *Thriving Youth Groups* was coming out, Jeanne and I had the privilege of leading a summit for youth leaders at the Group headquarters in Colorado.

Jeanne, who is married to a senior pastor, has more energy than a twelve-year-old, and she didn't get the memo that a middle-aged mom is not what a church needs to build a thriving youth ministry. She has grown ministries from a handful of students to over a thousand. When you ask her how, she will tell you that, after Jesus, nothing has affected the growth of her ministries like the climate of friendship that has been built there. Almost everything I know about how to build a friendship culture, I learned from Jeanne (or from other people who learned from Jeanne—including my own son—but more about that later).

I will certainly not do Jeanne's process justice here (for that, buy her book), but I do want to offer a simple outline of how a youth ministry might strategically create its own friendship epidemic.

Examine your process. The first step is to start by defining exactly what you want a first-time visitor or an "outsider" to experience at each of your ministry settings. For our ministry, we look at the Sunday-morning window from the time the student's car drives into the church parking lot until the time he or she gets back to it, including all of these steps:

- finding a parking spot

- getting out of the car

- figuring out where his or her group meets

- finding the right room

- stepping into the room

- getting connected to a "sticky friend"

- filling out a first-timer card

- finding a seat

- doing the program

- leaving with something

- leaving knowing how to find answers to questions about the youth ministry

- choosing to come another time

- feeling wanted after leaving

Now go back through this list and underline the two or three places where prospective students might decide never to come back. Then circle the one part of the process that tends to get the vast majority of our time and attention.

If you're like most youth workers, you circled the program. In fact, most of us spend 90 percent of our effort preparing the week's program (writing the curriculum, planning the games and so on). The truth is that the formal program is only one in a series of steps every student goes through. When we begin to think in terms of steps, not simply in terms of a program, we recognize our need to reallocate the time invested in the various steps.

Very few kids step out of a youth ministry because the programs are lousy. Kids will actually forgive all kinds of programmatic mediocrity *if* they are certain they belong. Consider what most teenagers do on weekend nights. They don't usually have brilliant, hypercreative plans (you've seen them meandering through Blockbuster for hours, looking for a movie to rent). They simply "hang out" with their friends. If our youth ministries don't provide students with the opportunity to be with the kinds of friends they want, it won't matter how spiritual, cutting-edge or outrageous our programs are; kids will not stick.

Make the shift from a program focus to a friendship focus. Think back to the *Group* survey. Remember what came last on the list? "A fast-paced, high-tech, entertaining ministry approach."

How often do kids walk into our "outreach programs," the ones designed to engage the outsider, to find the student and adult leaders scrambling around finishing the final setup, practicing for the skit or putting the final touches on the video or PowerPoint of the day?

With a program focus, the number-one priority is getting our programs right. With a friendship focus, we corral our program preparation time so that, if something has to slide, it won't be our availability to the lost or lonely student walking through the door.

In *Practicing Passion*, Kenda Dean identifies the three longings every teenager carries with him or her into every one of our youth meetings.

1. "Know me" (the longing for communion)

2. "Move me" (the longing for transcendence)

3. "Be there for me" (the longing for fidelity)

Though it could be argued that the adolescent longing for transcendence ("move me") requires a high-quality, moving program, it's important to remember that our students are much more likely to be *moved* relationally rather than programmatically. Some experts suggest that unless a newcomer has at least seven friends in the church, after six months, that student will be gone.

It's not that programs are irrelevant. They're simply secondary.

Cara Jenkins, now a youth worker in Sacramento, describes how youth group friendship took place in her own life:

> Large-group meetings merely lay down the groundwork, lower the drawbridge and tear down the walls so that life change can occur in more intimate settings. With a Postmodern mindset, *people in this emerging culture process truth relationally.*
>
> TIM CELEK AND DIETER ZANDER

When I was a sophomore in high school, I attended a youth group and was pretty cynical. I knew I came across pretty hard, and I didn't expect them to care or accept me. Not only were they friendly and warm, but when I came back a second week, they remembered my name! Now, every week, I search out those girls who think they won't fit in and love them like a few amazing people did for me when I was a teenager. I know it's easier to gravitate toward kids who look like they have it all together, but breaking down social barriers has to start with our example as leaders.

DEVELOP YOUR OWN EXTRAVAGANZA SQUAD

At this stage in the game, we don't recommend launching an official "student leadership program." We recommend focusing instead on identifying, developing and accessing students to engage in specific ministries for which they're uniquely gifted. I love the term my friend and veteran youth pastor Joe Cox uses for this process. He calls it "student apprenticeship" rather than student leadership, emphasizing that these young people are being mentored into service, not simply handed the reins of power.

When I'm looking for potential student apprentices, I *look down* to try to find people bending over to do the work that no one else wants to do (like picking up trash after youth group), and I look to the corners for the people who have a knack for paying attention to those at the fringes of the group. A little affirmation and a few assignments can go a long way toward empowering student apprentices, one at a time, long before a formal student apprentice program is put together.

One of my greatest thrills over the past three years was having my son Adam on the staff of our youth ministry as the high-school outreach director. During his short tenure, he championed (loudly and repeatedly) the priority that everyone who walks through the door of our youth ministry feel loved. He accomplished this priority primarily through the creation of The Extravaganza Squad (or ESquad for short).

Our Extravaganza Squad is a group of forty or so students who have taken as their responsibility the creation of a contagious friendship culture in every program of our youth ministry. Depending heavily on advice from Jeanne's book, Adam started by teaching the ESquad the difference between seeing new people as visitors and seeing new people as guests.

He asked the group to think about what it feels like to be on a visiting team at a sporting event and to describe the messages visitors get from the home team. The ESquad shouted out,

- "You don't belong."

- "We're gonna kick your tail."

- "We'll make you wish you'd never stepped into our school."

- "Go home!"

"Guests," on the other hand, are treated like royalty. When we have guests for dinner, we take out the best china and cook our best meals. When we're guests at a nice hotel, the "home team" is at our service, wanting to do everything they can to make our stay enjoyable. Isn't this the idea the author of Hebrews was getting at when he wrote, "Do not forget to entertain strangers, for by so doing some people have entertained angels without knowing it" (Heb 13:2)?

The ESquad owns the atmosphere for every guest; they own the responsibility for making every outsider student in the room feel like a VIP. Every Sunday school class also has a mini ESquad that meets fifteen minutes before the students start to arrive. In these meetings, the group celebrates the ways outsiders have been made to feel welcome during the previous week, identifies any fringe students who might need a little special attention and prays together.

Take time to train the team. The first step in training a team of students to create a magnetic friendship culture is to schedule enough time to bring everyone onboard to accomplish the initiative you're undertaking. We have seen too many "right" initiatives fail because there wasn't enough time allotted to get all the players moving in the same direction.

Once time has been scheduled (but not before then), you can begin the actual training. We like to start that training where Jeanne does—with Paul Revere.

In his bestselling book *The Tipping Point,* Malcolm Gladwell offers a fascinating investigation of how social epidemics happen, how a product or a behavior moves from being an isolated practice to being embraced by a much wider audience. In one of Gladwell's most memorable images, he describes the dramatic difference between the results experienced by Paul Revere and those experienced by a relatively unknown figure named William Dawes.

Both men were sent with the same message—to warn local militias to prepare for the British invasion that was coming in the morning. Those on the side of the river assigned to William Dawes seem to have received the message and then rolled over and fallen right back to sleep, while those alerted by Paul Revere sprung to life, with the warning spreading like wildfire to the surrounding villages and farms. The message was exactly the same, but the results couldn't have been more different.

When Jeanne brings her leadership group of students together, she begins with this story and makes the purpose crystal-clear with this introduction:

> So why did I ask you to show up tonight? I guess I want you to know that I view each of you as Paul Reveres in a world full of William Dawes. You have the ability to influence the people around you. I'm asking you to use that influence to create a revolution of authentic friendship in [our group]. . . .
>
> I'm asking you to be a part of an unofficial leadership team on Wednesday nights. I know that if the people in this room are on my team, together we can dramatically change the tenor of our whole youth ministry. None of us want this to be just a holy huddle.

Once the group is clear on its purpose, they're assigned specific tasks. Some ESquad students are to greet everyone who comes through the door; some are to connect with people at the food table; others serve as "row hosts," greeting everyone who sits in their section; others stay at the welcome table to give a gift to every newcomer; and still others work at a game area to help provide an active focal point particularly for hyperkinetic junior high boys.

Many churches that make friendship central to the DNA of their youth ministry continue to provide for the training of their student apprentices. One church asks their friendship-epidemic students each to create their Most Wanted List of five inactive students for whom they will pray regularly. Whenever the youth ministry sponsors an outreach event, everyone is expected to invite two of the five. They aren't responsible for whether or not those students come, but they are responsible to invite them.

Other churches take time with their student-apprentice team each year to specifically attack what Jeanne names as the two most dangerous, community-killing viruses in youth ministry: gossip and sarcasm.

Still other churches encourage their ESquad students to approach the pursuit of outsiders as an intentional spiritual practice, as a part of the way disciples live out their faith. To do this, students visit other youth groups, as the outsiders, to learn from both those who welcome them well and those who fail to do so.

SUSTAINING A FRIENDSHIP CULTURE

If our ministry has a clique problem, it's because we've structured it to give cliques too much power. If we have an apathy problem, it may be that we're creating bored consumers. If our eleventh- and twelfth-graders are dropping out of sight, could it be that we've structured our ministry in such a way that this result is inevitable?

I want to be clear that the *idea* of creating a friendship culture doesn't work. We have to work the processes of friendship culture. These processes keep key stakeholders focused on a shared commitment to community until those practices become almost imperceptibly imbedded into the DNA of the group. Though there are certainly more, we choose to access three of these core practices in our ministry.

1. *The Deuteronomy 6 retreat.* We need more than weekly youth meetings if we hope to move from being a "youth group" to being a "youth family." Becoming family comes from time together, with some suggesting that it takes a minimum of eight hours of "face time" before a group of people can *begin* to experience community.

Remember Deuteronomy 6:4-9, the *Shema*. In these few verses, God gives his people a clear strategy for passing on their faith to the next generation (and hiring a youth director was never mentioned!). Moses identified four specific, high-leverage settings in which the passing on of God's love to the next generation was most likely to happen.

See if you can find the four in the text:

Hear, O Israel: The LORD our God, the LORD is one. Love the LORD your God with all your heart and with all your soul and with all your strength. These commandments that I give you today are to be upon your hearts. Impress them on your children. Talk about them when you sit at home and when you walk along the road, when you lie down and when you get up. Tie them as symbols on your hands and bind them on your foreheads. Write them on the doorframes of your houses and on your gates. (Deut 6:4-9)

Moses gave God's people specific times when they were to talk with the younger generation about the love of God: "when you sit at home and when you walk along the road, when you lie down and when you get up," all four of which happen on retreats and trips. It's on these over-night experiences that all four of the Deuteronomy 6 moments happen, when we begin and end our days together, eat meals together and take a journey together.

2. The ballad of the bard. Almost every time Adam met with the E-Squad, he told a tale, typically a tale of one of its members going above and beyond. As the "bard" of the ESquad, Adam's stories shaped the identity of the group, reminding them that *they* were the ones who were successfully taking away the awkward edge for a self-conscious new-comer (or for an old-timer who hasn't yet found his or her niche).

Somewhere in the first few meetings, the ESquad came up with a motto that captured this responsibility perfectly: "We feel awkward so you don't have to!"

Each time the ESquad gathers (usually in the hour before a major event or a monthly outreach), their most consistent ritual is "stack-ing it up" (like an athletic team might before a game) and shouting their motto in unison: "We feel awkward so you don't have to!" Ritu-als like this are all a part of the bard role that youth workers play with student leaders.

When it comes to telling the stories that create a magnetic friendship culture, Jeanne is the poet laureate. Here's an example of the kinds of truth she sings into the lives of her students:

We all come from different backgrounds. Some of us attend [high school A], others attend [high school B]. Some of us come from families with lots of money and others of us have to work hard to make ends meet. None of that matters in this place. The ground is level here for everyone.

Some of us are football heroes, and others of us are computer nerds. It doesn't matter if you're a prep, geek, jock, or nothing. We're just glad to have you!

We are not as much a youth group as we are a youth family. Whether this is your first time here or your millionth, we're really glad to have you.

We can't assume that these ideas will be obvious to everyone who walks through the doors of our ministry. While we're ostensibly talking to the new people, every time the bard gets up to speak, he or she reminds regular youth, who once again remember, "Oh yeah, that's who we are."

3. The follow-up process. When a person visits for the first time, we want him or her to walk away feeling *wanted, accepted* and *connected.* Though the accomplishment of this goal is highly dependent on what happens at our program, we can take crucial steps after the visit to confirm our interest.

The first follow-up habit is a brief letter, ideally sent the day after the newcomer's visit. In the letter, we reaffirm how glad we are that they attended the event, tell them just a bit about our ministry, invite them back and assure them that, if they're involved in another church, they're welcome to attend our youth group without feeling pressure to change churches. At the bottom of the letter, one of our youth staff writes a personal note. The letter is then stamped (not run through the postage meter) and hand-addressed (instead of using a mailing label) before it's sent.

Our second follow-up habit is a phone call from one of the members of the ESquad. Calls are assigned by grade and sometimes by school, with the ESquad members trained to say again how glad we are about the visit and to ask for helpful feedback, using a statement something like this: "We're really trying to get feedback from everyone who visits with us. We always like to find out if there's anything we could have done that would've made your visit with us more what you had hoped it would be. Do you have any input for us?"

The final follow-up habit is our MIA list. Every month, we generate a list of all the students who haven't attended in the past month.

Typically, we divide this list among our youth staff, who leave check-in messages, talk to parents, and every now and then actually talk to students. Though some churches try to assign these tasks to volunteers, it's our strong opinion that these calls belong primarily to the staff. Here's why:

- Calls to inactive folks tend to be the most difficult. A volunteer making these calls is likely to feel overwhelmed and powerless to make the kinds of changes that might make an MIA student want to come back.

- A call from a staff person raises the stakes; the parents and the student feel that someone "important" really does notice him or her.

- When youth staff get honest feedback from someone who has dropped out, they get a clearer picture of the most urgent priorities from those who are on the outside of the ministry.

STUDENT LEADERSHIP IN PERSPECTIVE

One message we often hear in an assessment or visioning process is "all we really need to do is let the kids run the program." "After all," the argument goes, "it's their program." The folks making these recommendations might be great youth leaders, but they're lousy historians.

According to youth ministry historian Mark Senter, "student movements led by students below the college level are *absent* from the annals of youth ministry." In other words, the idea of student leadership that many well-meaning leaders are suggesting has *never* happened, at least not in documented history.

"Letting the kids do it" eventually devolves into monthly committee meetings with students, focusing on scheduling and complaining. Other churches blithely assume that if they can get more teenagers to serve on adult committees, those students will naturally be attracted to leadership in the church as adults, and their committees will make youth-friendly decisions. I've never seen it happen. The truth is that an effective, well-designed, strategically implemented student apprenticeship program is one of the most complex and problematic pieces of a thriving youth ministry.

Please understand. I'm a fan of youth in leadership. Nothing has influenced the climate of our ministry and the attentiveness of our younger students quite like the juniors and seniors serving in apprentice roles. Though there are certain ministries that can *only* be accomplished by students, deciding whether to go bowling or play laser tag is not one of them.

Because so many youth ministries get tripped up in trying to build their student leadership team too early, let me identify quickly what a quality student apprenticeship program *is not:*

- It's not quickly cobbling together a group of kids to lead because some expert says "youth-driven" youth ministry works.

- It's not giving kids responsibility for setting the direction of the youth ministry.

- It's not having adults step out of the way so kids can take responsibility for the ministry.

- It's not getting kids together to decide what events they want to put on the youth group calendar.

Those who believe that student leadership in youth ministry is simply about adults getting out of the way so kids can take over are wrong-headed and short-sighted. Their brain genes have been doused with the same sort of laughing gas that led French philosopher Rousseau to conclude that the problem with education is . . . ADULTS! *If we tyrannical adults would just leave children alone they would learn, grow, and develop just fine on their own. Like wild flowers in a meadow, kids have everything they need to bloom their way toward a beautiful life. Only adults could mess up such a naturally perfect plan. . . .*

Poppycock.

DAVE RAHN

- It's not getting kids together to tell the youth staff how well they're doing their jobs.

Some are under the illusion that using student leaders is easier than adults taking the lead. The opposite is usually true. If a church hopes to save time or is having trouble recruiting adults, that church needs to let go of the illusion that a thriving student leadership program will somehow take *less* time.

The most profound student leadership programs happen not when students are asked to plan the calendar or evaluate the quality of this or that program, as a student council might. Traditional approaches to student leadership might give students power, but they fail at a basic level. They fail to provide students with the life-on-life, uncomfortable ministry experiences that allow them to feel awkward enough to inspire their growth and effectively catalyze a culture of welcome in their youth ministries.

12

DANCING WITH ALLIGATORS

Navigating the Turbulent Waters of Church Politics

Religion is a big, beautiful, ugly thing. I read recently where Augustine said, "The church is a whore and it is my mother." And for reasons I don't understand, Jesus loves the church. And I suppose He loves the church with the same strength of character He displays in His love for me. Sometimes it is difficult to know which is the greater miracle.

DONALD MILLER

Every departmental silo in any company can ultimately be traced back to the leaders of those departments, who have failed to understand the dependencies that must exist among the executive team, or who have failed to make those interdependencies clear to the people deeper in their departments.

PATRICK LENCIONI

After twenty years leading youth ministry at the same church, I've earned what I call an "involuntary doctorate" in church politics. I wasn't trying to be a good church politician. In fact, the whole concept of church politics was as distasteful to me as it is to most youth ministers.

I had always viewed church politics as a way for powerful and clever people to take advantage of the rest of us. I saw it as a way for high-powered people to push their agendas, which usually meant cutting a few sleazy backroom deals with cloak-and-dagger efficiency. I enjoyed a good Dilbert cartoon as much as the next guy.

But after hitting lots of brick walls, after a long series of painful failures in ministry, I now recognize that church politics is no laughing matter. The success of our youth ministry is inextricably tied to and, at times, dependent on, people and groups in our church over which the youth ministry has no control.

The finance committee determines what our annual youth budget is. The facilities team determines the availability of space for our youth programs. The senior staff and the elders either affirm or block our plans for strategic growth. I realized that if I didn't learn a little about church politics, our ministry would always walk with a limp.

I've been blessed to be surrounded by a wide assortment of leaders—in business, in medicine and in the church—who redefined for me what church politics might mean. They taught me that, far from being slimy and deceitful, church politics is—surprisingly—about relationships and respect.

As I was discovering some of these principles in the curriculum cauldron of my own mistakes, I came across a study that investigated the role office politics play in people losing their jobs. By interviewing workers who, when dismissed from their positions, pointed to office politics as the cause, the researchers hoped to come to a clear definition of exactly what "office politics" meant. As they dug a little deeper and analyzed data from the interviews, they made an amazing discovery: what the disgruntled workers described as "politics" boiled down to little more than *relationships,* the regular give-and-take interaction with other people. The researchers summed up their discoveries this way:

> Most careers involve other people. You can have great academic
> intelligence and still lack social intelligence—the ability to be a

good listener, to be sensitive toward others, to give and take criticism well.

If people don't like you, they may *help* you fail. . . . On the other hand, you can get away with serious mistakes if you are socially intelligent. . . . A mistake may actually *further* [your] career if the boss thinks [you] handled the situation in a mature and responsible way.

In a study of 185 youth pastors who'd been fired from their jobs, 42 percent had actually *grown* their youth groups numerically in the previous year. They were fired not because of their failure to produce results but, quite likely, because of their failure to accomplish these results without alienating key stakeholders.

I don't want to minimize the pain some youth ministers have experienced at the hands of pathological leaders, of which the church certainly has its fair share. But I do wonder if many of the "horror stories" we hear about the ways elders and senior pastors have treated youth ministers are about a failure to communicate.

> I would lean close to you at our fast-food restaurant meeting and say very firmly, "If you want to be an effective leader, you must learn to deal with relational conflict. There is no getting around this one. Resolving conflict is part of leadership."
>
> DOUG FIELDS

PAGES FROM A POLITICAL BUNGLER'S JOURNAL

Because my understanding of the ins and outs of church politics came primarily through trial and error (more error than trial), I'll start by describing a few of my own failures and then identify the key components every sustainable youth ministry will, eventually, need to have in place.

Bungle 1: Isolationism. Early in my ministry, I believed that my job was to focus exclusively on our youth ministry. I didn't want to be distracted by issues like worship attendance, stewardship or family camp. But then I read the Bible. And I read these very inconvenient words from early in Philippians: "Do nothing out of selfish ambition or vain conceit, but in humility consider others better than yourselves. Each of you should look not only to your own interests, but also to the interests of others" (2:3-4). Though I don't need to become entangled in other ministries of the church, I realize now that my apathy about those ministries was far from faithful.

I've met too many youth workers who secretly smile when they see the failure of the staid and stodgy music department. Too many of us offer only self-satisfied silence when parents or youth complain about how boring the worship service is. One (recently unemployed) youth pastor gave his entire tithe to the youth ministry he was leading, rather than to the church. When we approach our ministry as if it's the only thing that matters, we perpetuate the illusion that the different parts of the church are in different boats that float or sink independently, rather than recognizing that we're all in one big boat.

There's a whole lot more to youth ministry than youth ministry. A hole in the boat sinks all of us, even those of us on the other side of the boat.

Bungle 2: Following my own passion first. Within two years of stepping into my role as a youth pastor in Nashville, I became fascinated with the idea of family-based youth ministry. Over the next six years, I made it my priority to think through, craft and launch this new way of thinking about and doing youth ministry. I was following my passion.

The only problem was that the church hadn't hired me to follow my passion. It had not hired me to develop a new model for ministry. The church had called me to engage the youth of our congregation in a magnetic ministry that would lead them toward deeper maturity in Christ, toward lives of service, deeply connected with this particular body of Christ.

If I had to do it over again, would I still do family-based youth ministry? Absolutely. Our ministry is now thoroughly family-based. I'm grateful for the privilege of leading with a model I obviously believe in so much.

But I realize now that I could have spent just as much time developing a more family-based approach if I hadn't *talked* about it so much (and hadn't used it as an excuse for not doing the work I was hired to do). If I could do it over again, I'd give my first attention to the specific work to which I'd been called, persistently pursuing my senior pastor to confirm that I was moving toward priorities at the top of *his* list.

The more stories I listen to, the more I see how often youth workers hamstring themselves by following their own passions. I recently read in a *Youthworker* article by Suzi Woodrow about a youth minister who spent all his time with kids on the beach or surfing with kids. Not surprisingly, the elders of the church let him go. If he had been hired explicitly to reach out to kids on the beach, fabulous! I have little doubt that his ministry there was fruitful. But too many youth workers focus their energy on something other than the jobs they were hired to do and then are shocked to discover the leaders of the church all over their backs.

> Most church people have the nerve to believe that our job . . . is to first reach the church kids. . . . If we have no heart for our churched kids, we had better find a different ministry. . . . I'm not saying we need to automatically bail out of church-based youth ministry if we have a heart for the lost. I am saying integrity demands that we bail if we have no heart for the found.
>
> LEN KAGELER

Bungle 3: The porcupine party. Recently I heard the church described as a group of porcupines. As the world becomes threatening on the outside, we do two things simultaneously: we put out our protective quills, and we move closer to each other. It's not long before we hurt each other in our efforts at self-protection. When that pain gets too intense, we wander off in isolation to deal with those fearful threats, but this time, we are alone.

Many of the mistakes I've made with church politics have been driven *not* by my desire to build a thriving ministry but by my own anxious heart. Because I feel threatened in some way, I turn to any number of porcupine reactions. These reactions do little to build the youth ministry or the church as a whole, and eventually they diminish me, not only in the eyes of those whose opinion I value, but in my own eyes as well. When I'm "losing" at the game of church politics, it's all too easy to turn to one of these porcupine reactions:

Nose knocking: "I don't mean to be mean, but the guy before me . . ." The most notable characteristic of the Great Sphinx of Giza is not its location next to the pyramids; it's not its 240-foot lion's body with the head of a man. It's that the face has no nose. Ancient leaders discredited positive memory of other rulers by defacing sculptures built in their honor. Although today we see those Vandal kings as weak, too many who claim to lead in the way of Christ still find it necessary to knock off the noses of their predecessors.

Manure bombs: "There's nothing to talk about. I've said everything in my email." I've borrowed the "manure bomb" idea from Thom and Joani Schultz, who warn us,

> Confrontational notes and e-mails are akin to manure bombs. To the receiver, they come out of nowhere, allow no defense, do nasty damage, and provoke retaliatory bombings. Written missiles, lacking the nuances of voice inflection and facial expressions, are often misconstrued. And they allow no opportunity for concurrent give-and-take. They're simply unfair, cowardly sucker punches. When you have something difficult to say, do it in person.

Pole-vaulting over rat droppings: "I don't mean this as a threat, but if this new policy about the blue pens sticks, I'll be looking for another position." In a porcupine culture, battles over nonessentials can escalate to the point of threats that are way out of proportion to the issue. Peter Scazzero identifies five unhealthy ways of dealing with conflict in the church that are used more often than we'd like to admit:

- escalation

- withdrawal

- attack

- assuming things are worse than reality

- "triangulating" (talking through a third person rather than dealing directly with the person involved in the conflict)

Using any of these tactics can leverage a debate over an insignificant issue into a trust-breaking grudge that cripples communication for years.

Conflict avoidance: "That's fine." Many churches produce such a "culture of niceness" that the leaders avoid engaging in the critical disagreement that's essential for its own health. Too many churches confuse peace-faking with peacemaking, and conflict moves from the leaders meeting into the parking lot, where previously silent people of like mind gather around their cars to say what they really think.

> **Harmony sometimes restricts "productive ideological conflict," the passionate interchange of opinions around an issue.**
>
> **PATRICK LENCIONI**

Youth workers who miss the point of the porcupine warning eventually find themselves skewered by their own anxious reactions. Porcupine-like self-protection simply doesn't work.

THE UNSPOKEN RULES OF CHURCH POLITICS

After a youth director runs into brick wall after brick wall in the world of church politics, too often he or she simply resorts to complaining, the most popular youth worker weapon of choice. But I would like to suggest an alternative: learning.

To learn the unique traditions and political processes of your church, look at them like an anthropologist trying to learn the unspoken processes for decision making in a particular culture. Try looking at processes in the same way you might learn the unique mealtime culture of a particular family. These processes are not good or bad, they just *are.* If you hope to enjoy your stay with this family, you'll learn them as well.

Though every church has its unique culture and informal approval processes, there are some universal rules of church politics.

Access internal marketing. We all know what marketing is: getting the word out about who you are and what you have to offer to your "customers." But *internal* marketing is different. The target of internal marketing is not our customers, but our colleagues and any others who might have a stake in the success of the youth ministry, including church officers, potential leaders and alumni youth and parents.

Because you're reading this book, there's a good chance you're seen as an ambassador for your youth ministry. If you're the senior pastor, periodically mentioning the youth of the church in sermons is internal marketing. If you're a volunteer leader, talking to a church friend over coffee about a recent happening in the youth ministry is internal marketing. If you're the youth director, introducing leadership students to some of the leaders of the church is internal marketing. Articles in the church newsletter and the bulletin are (you guessed it) internal marketing. In the language of Proverbs 22:1, you're helping to establish "a good name" for the youth ministry.

The simplest internal marketing process starts with discovering the primary pet peeve of your supervisor—and addressing it appropriately. One senior pastor evaluates the quality of the youth ministry by the order in the youth pastor's office. Another addresses his pet peeve in the monthly youth newsletter. Another wants check requests or reports turned in on time. Youth workers who ignore their senior pastor's pet peeves pour salt into a wounded relationship and eventually find themselves in an uphill climb every time they need approval (or funding) for a new idea.

Decisions in the church, like decisions in any organization, are based at least partly on the gut sense people have about the department (or the leader of the department) in question. If my elders have heard very little about the goings-on of the youth ministry over the past year, they're much slower to respond positively to the specific request I'm bringing to the table.

Learn the fine art of keeping your supervisor on your team. In *Your First Two Years in Youth Ministry,* Doug Fields gives new youth workers some of the best advice I've ever heard about working with senior pastors:

- "*Trust.* This is what a senior pastor desires in a youth worker. Someone who can be en*trust*ed with an entire area of ministry. Someone who will lead it well. Someone you don't have to worry about."

- "While some personalities are controlling, most senior pastors I've met or heard about don't want to manage you. They don't have time. They want to *trust* you, believing that you'll do the job you were hired to do and that you'll support and practice the church's philosophy of ministry."

- "My philosophy about working with a senior pastor is to do whatever I can to make his life easier."

Trust is our most valuable currency for dealing with senior leadership. And trust, as we know, takes a long time to build and only seconds to destroy. A single ignored assignment, a single delayed response, a single expression of gossip about the senior pastor to someone else on the church staff, and the value of our currency diminishes exponentially.

Just a few months ago, my senior pastor, Todd Jones, gave me the most powerful words of encouragement I've ever heard from a boss. In the annual review with the chair of the personnel committee, he said something like this: "I know I can *trust* you. I know the kinds of things you say to people about me. I know your commitment to seeing our whole church succeed, not just your little piece of it."

I'm not suggesting perfection. What I'm suggesting is that, when we blow it with our senior pastor (or with others to whom we have a reporting relationship), we immediately and without excuses accept responsibility and ask forgiveness, knowing that the way we handle our failures can itself be an opportunity to build trust.

It's helpful for every youth worker to learn his or her boss's preferred style of communication. One supervisor may want daily updates with numbers by email, another might be looking for stories every week on voicemail, and a third might ask for a written monthly report. But all senior staff appreciate being asked for their advice every now and then, whether it's about a new person being hired, a new initiative being tried, or a particularly complex problem with a volunteer or a student.

Though we don't want to flood our boss's inbox or voicemail with information, overcommunicating is better than keeping him or her in the dark. When we make it one of our ministry goals never to set our senior pastors up to be surprised, we save untold hours of repair work later.

Cast the net wide before initiating change. Thanks to the vision of our senior pastor and eighteen months of infrastructure building, our youth ministry was months away from launching what was to become the Center for Youth Ministry Training (CYMT), a bold, extensive initiative involving church leaders in finances, facilities and mission.

To make matters more complex, this effort was being launched in collaboration with Brentwood United Methodist Church, the Institute for Youth Ministry at Princeton Theological Seminar, the Youth Academy at Duke Divinity School and the Cal Turner Center for Church Leadership at Martin Methodist College.

Though the general plan had received enthusiastic support from our elders, I was beginning to hear reports that a number of them had grave concerns about the long-term implications of this plan. So I paid a visit to one of our key elders, a long-time friend and a wise and thorough businessman, to ask for his advice. He happily shared his concerns about the project, which we resolved together with surprising speed.

Before I left, he gave me invaluable advice: "There are a good number of other people you need to have meetings like this with before this thing comes up for a vote." Together we made a list of elders I should visit, and I spent much of the rest of that week in those meetings, capped off with a follow-up meeting with Todd. The elders approved the proposal unanimously, and in the fall of 2006, the CYMT was launched.

Determining our most important priorities is not enough (though, according to some estimates, more than 97 percent of people fail to do even that much). When we have a key initiative (as complex as the CYMT or as seemingly simple as changing the format of Sunday school), we've got to move beyond just having a plan. We've got to get the right people on board with the plan, listen to their concerns and adjust our plans as necessary.

Write the last great chapter for your critics. Laurence Steinberg studied 204 families with adolescents in Wisconsin. Apart from the single shared characteristic of having teenagers, these families were very diverse: urban, white, black, suburban, rural, single-parent, remarried and so on. One truth that bubbled up: "Teenagers can make you crazy."

The study revealed that "40% of the study parents showed a decline in psychological well-being during their children's adolescence." Steinberg suggested that what has come to be known as the "midlife crisis" may be more related to having teenagers in the house than to the physical effects of aging. In fact, the forty-something parent with a teenager is much less likely to be psychologically healthy and to feel good about his or her marriage than the same-age parent with a seven-year-old.

I am not offering this study as an excuse for youth workers to dismiss the criticism of "crazy" parents. What I'm suggesting is that the parents of the youth we work with need our support, sometimes desperately. Too many youth workers respond to parental criticism more out of defensiveness than compassion.

When a parent sees us in the hall at church and says, "You're going on vacation *again*? You just had a week off at camp," our tendency is to respond defensively, with a politically incorrect response like, "Why don't *you* try taking a week at camp and see if it feels like a vacation to *you?!*"

For some criticism—like the one raised by this parent—there is no "right answer." What we can do, though, is respond with the right spirit, without reacting negatively, recognizing that the one taking the pot-shots is likely speaking out of his or her own pain.

The truth is, criticism gives us the opportunity to write "the last great chapter." Here's how it can work:

Let's imagine you go to a restaurant, and you receive less than mediocre service. Then imagine that you take the time to write a letter to the management and give them a piece of your mind. You let them know in no uncertain terms that you've decided never to return to this establishment.

But then you get a letter from the manager, followed by multiple phone calls from the corporate office, along with fifty dollars in coupons for future meals. Each call thanks you for your input, assuring you that the restaurant wants to do anything it can to keep you as a valued customer and friend. Most of us would not only go back, we'd also tell all our friends about the attention we received.

Complaints are often thinly veiled opportunities for us to show our willingness to listen to those we've been called to serve.

Nobody likes criticism. But when we're criticized, too many of us resort to avoidance and defensiveness. Instead of staying in the uncomfortable place of listening and reconciliation, we postpone responding to our critics' calls and emails, which of course only makes them more critical.

Ordinarily, the ministry instincts of a youth staff person are right. But sometimes we miss it (like when one of our staff people sponsored a middle-school boys' video-game night using M-rated games, which many of our parents prohibited their sons from playing). Unless we're careful, when we're being criticized, we make it our first priority to "make our point."

But our true first priority is to hear the concern of the critic, listen for the nugget of wisdom and search for creative solutions together. Sometimes when I'm criticized, I start feeling so defensive that I have to buy myself time by saying something like, "I hear your concern, and it's so important that I want to talk it through with my senior pastor before moving immediately to a solution."

Does this mean we always have to yield to our critics? If we truly believe that youth ministries are most effective when they support parents, we would be wise to set our default button such that we ordinarily defer to parents.

Of course, there will be times when we'll need to stand like a rock. But if we're "willing to die" over the time youth group meets or the attendance requirements for confirmation, we may be more like the three-year-old reacting to the crisis of an empty box of Cocoa Puffs than like a leader who knows how and when to stand with conviction.

WARNING: QWERTY AHEAD

In 1874, the Sholes & Glidden Type Writer was the best typewriter around. The creators discovered that some typists had a problem. They typed so fast that the strike keys locked up, so they created a keyboard designed to *slow* fingers down (for example, pinky fingers do *a* and *p*), what we now know as the QWERTY keyboard. Even though other keyboards have increased typing speed by as much as 50 perecent, those new keyboards have never been accepted.

Change is not all about logic. And wise change agents in the church recognize that some initiatives, no matter how logical and right, are just fighting a QWERTY culture. There are battles that can't be won.

As far back as 1996, 1,300 ministers a month in the United States were fired or forced to resign. Nearly 30 percent of ministers have been terminated at least once. A decade from now, it is estimated that 40 percent of today's pastors will be in another line of work.

Most of these pastors are brilliant, compassionate, faithful men and women, godly leaders trained in the study of Scripture, in thinking theologically and in providing care for those struggling with their faith or with a personal crisis. But few of us were ever told that to survive in the church, we must be experts at navigating the turbulent waters of church politics.

The time has come for those responsible for youth ministry to take responsibility for galvanizing the support of stakeholders in the youth ministry beyond the small circle of those actively involved in our program. To accomplish such a thing, we need to become adept at the last skill we thought we would need in ministry: church politics.

13

RABBIT TRAILS AND BRICK WALLS

When All the Brilliant Plans Don't Work

Success is never final.
WINSTON CHURCHILL

"Spontaneity" is often mistaken for "fresh." Instead of fresh ministry served thoughtfully with a balanced program of Bible study, small groups and relationships—basically, a ministry driven by biblical purpose—we believe that fresh is just "letting the Sprit lead." Fresh becomes "whatever happens, happens." But that's not fresh programming; it's half-baked programming.

Someday, take a look at the supplementary DVD material for *The Lord of the Rings* trilogy. You'll discover all kinds of fascinating facts:

- All three movies were shot at the same time in New Zealand using three different film crews.

- The three Tolkien books were boiled down to a single ninety-page story that was then story boarded and first animated.

- Parts of the movie were first filmed in rough form, using local actors before the stars ever showed up for filming.

But the most fascinating fact is that, in spite of all this intense preparation, the script was actually *rewritten* almost every night. Most mornings, the actors woke up to discover a brand new version of the day's script under their door.

I love the image one of the writers used in one of the interviews. He compared the whole process to *laying down tracks just a few yards ahead of a moving train*. Now *there's* an accurate picture of sustainable youth ministry! In spite of all our plans and preparations, the best youth ministries are continually working and improving their plans, rewriting the script every day, laying tracks just a few yards ahead of the train.

WHY MOST STRATEGIC PLANS DON'T WORK

We were wrapping up a recent visioning retreat, with the twenty or so youth ministry stakeholders completely exhausted and totally energized at the same time. As we stood in a circle to pray ourselves home, one of the women asked me, "Okay, when are you going to tell us?" I tilted my head like a puzzled puppy.

She said, "You guys see this stuff all the time. When are you going to tell us the right way?"

I understood what she was asking for. She believed that there was a secret formula, a "right" model for building a thriving youth ministry. Fortunately, the answer to her question was just outside the classroom window. Pointing to the massive church-building project underway, I said, "That's how you'll do it. Tonight we have finished drafting our blueprint; now we work the plan. And if we do it right, it will be a long, slow, messy, inconvenient process."

When a youth ministry begins the implementation of its strategic plans, those involved need to be prepared for an avalanche of speed bumps, rabbit trails and brick walls that will interrupt their progress. We've seen churches with great enthusiasm about their plans rush into their first good idea, slam into a brick wall and abandon their plans altogether. One of the biggest obstacles churches face in implementing their strategic youth ministry plans is that they expect every step of those plans to "work." But sustainable youth ministries sustain *a process*.

In the early years of Youth Ministry Architects, I focused almost exclusively on helping churches create their strategic youth ministry plans, like an architect providing a blueprint to a client. Every time I'd present these customized plans, I could tell by the nodding heads that the stakeholders clearly wanted to see these plans implemented.

But then I'd check in six months later. And I'd discover that the game plan that had generated so much enthusiasm was now filed away like a priceless historical artifact at the end of an Indiana Jones movie. Little or nothing was being done to translate the plan into reality. It was then that Youth Ministry Architects changed its focus—from being a document preparation team to becoming partners in the process of building sustainable youth ministries.

> **No plan will work unless you do.**
>
> **JEANNE MAYO**

Over the years, we've identified the rabbit trails that cause youth ministries to wander off their strategic course and pursue second, third or fourth priorities before attending to the first ones. It seems appropriate to end this book with a dose of realism, a picture of some of the temptations that can so easily derail any building process. Churches that invest sideways energy running down these rabbit trails will find themselves in the same place one, two, three years later, having wasted their time in the creation of a blueprint that has become little more than an exercise in fiction writing.

THOSE TEMPTING RABBIT TRAILS

Quick! Let's get to "the next level!" Hang around youth ministers long enough, and you'll soon hear someone talking about "the next level." Some were hired to "take their ministry to the next level." Some will tell you they're in the process of getting their ministry "to the next level." But most have no idea what "the next level" is, other than that it's got to be a whole lot more fun than the boring "first level" stuff.

Let's do it like Young Life (or the Methodists or the Catholics or the Baptists down the street). Deciding on a specific model for a youth ministry tends to come later in the building process and will likely morph over the years. It's common in an assessment or visioning retreat for one or more of the participants to obsess over the "tried and true" model that some other ministry is using. This is a rabbit trail that causes churches to decide that they simply *must* have a youth basketball program, a visitation program or any number of other programs that will only serve to stuff the calendar, exhaust volunteers and burn out staff.

> Creativity gets a very bad name when creative people always make a point of solving a different problem from the one they have been given.
>
> EDWARD de BONO

Let's build a building or buy more technology. Building facilities and accessing great technology, two of the most popular rabbit trails, are clearly "next-level" stuff. We've seen thriving youth ministries in mighty shabby facilities, and we've seen flat-lining youth ministries in state-of-the-art facilities. Great facilities and great technology can increase the momentum of a youth ministry, but they can't create it.

Otherwise very intelligent, articulate people say, with all sincerity, "The reason our kids don't want to be involved is because we don't have a gym." A church where kids don't feel welcome without a gym will not be able to make them feel welcome with one.

In the same way, we've seen more than our share of youth workers who've become technology experts, who (often because of their age) wind up doubling as the IT experts for the entire church. These youth workers love to chase the rabbits of making movies, building websites, installing software and sound equipment—all fine second- and third-level activities. But if the youth director "has no time" to attend to the foundational priorities identified in the last twelve chapters, the ministry is almost certain to stall before it ever launches.

Let's keep adding stuff to the calendar. It's funny how churches with floundering ministries overstuff their youth ministry calendars. If Sunday school isn't working, they add youth group. If those two aren't working, they add small groups. If Sunday school, small group and youth group don't seem to attract kids, they add a youth choir or a monthly special event or . . .

Like piling large, wet logs on a sputtering fire, piling more programs on a flailing youth ministry will likely extinguish whatever fire there is. Youth ministries, like fires, are very fragile at the beginning—starting with small pieces of easily ignitable wood gets the fire started. And once the fire is blazing, the larger stuff can be added. One of the hazards of all the great youth ministry "ideas" available today is that most youth workers have a knee-jerk tendency to implement a whole lot more of those ideas than they realistically have the capacity for.

SCALING THE BRICK WALL:
OVERCOMING THE INSURMOUNTABLE

Most youth ministers would say they have some sort of *plan*. Sometimes the plan gets sidetracked due to rabbit trails. But at other times, even after investing appropriately, visioning clearly and staying away from common rabbit trails, a youth ministry finds itself running into the same brick wall(s) over and over again.

Making it through the brick walls starts with accepting the fact that, as our ministries become sustainable, there will always be walls that stand in the way of moving forward strategically. When we recognize that brick walls are simply a part of ministry, we can stop beating ourselves up for being stuck and begin working a very specific process to scale those walls. To introduce this process, I'll tell the story of Lesleigh, an imaginary youth pastor who found a way to "scale the wall" of small groups.

For years, the youth ministry at First Church had talked about small groups. Lesleigh, the church's only youth staff person, would come up with grand ideas about small groups, launch them with great fanfare, but within weeks find that the new-and-improved small-group program was no more effective than that of the year before.

Lesleigh knew it wasn't working, so she pulled together three wise counselors, all committed to the youth ministry (but not serving in a specific role). She asked them to meet with her regularly until they had together "scaled" the small-group problem. She explained that she was looking for a commitment to two kinds of meetings: weekly one-hour tactical meetings to work the plans they developed and periodic three- to four-hour strategic meetings to develop or revise those plans (see chapter nine).

The group started with a four-hour strategic orientation at the home of a team member. They shared a meal and shared their dreams for a thriving small-group ministry. They put in writing a descriptive vision of what a sustainable small-group ministry might look like. They identified a game plan and a timeline for making their dreams a reality. Before the meeting was over, each person was given the same assignment: find at least one thriving small-group program and talk to the leader to discover transferable principles.

In the first weekly meeting, only two of the four team members had made their calls, one of them being Lesleigh. She pleasantly asked if her expectations were realistic, giving each person on the team a "get out of jail free card," the chance to bow out if he or she simply didn't have time.

One of the team members took the card. She explained that, though she loved the youth ministry and Lesleigh, she simply didn't have the time she'd thought she did. The meeting ended with everyone receiving the assignment to contact two of the current small-group leaders to gain insight into why previous attempts at building the small-group program had failed.

After finding a replacement for the lost team member, Lesleigh called all others before the meeting to check on their process. All four came prepared, and full of ideas. But not all the ideas were the same.

In fact, there was a sharp divide between two members: one wanted kids to be in groups with their friends, while the other wanted to break up cliques and mix the friendship groups. To make matters more complex, a third person wanted all the groups to be single-gender, while another wanted most, if not all, of the groups to be coed.

When the team seemed deadlocked, Lesleigh suggested that they make this issue the focus of their next strategic meeting. Again they all left with an assignment: contact three youth and three parents to glean their insight about how to structure the groups.

At the next monthly strategic meeting (this one lasting three hours), Lesleigh helped the team look at their conflict points through a variety of lenses (based on Edward de Bono's *Six Thinking Hats*). They resolved their questions by agreeing to an experimental game plan: they would recruit eight small-group leaders to launch four different six-week exploratory small groups:

1. an existing coed friendship cluster

2. a coed collection of youth who barely knew each other

3. an all-girls group

4. an all-boys group

They agreed that this was an experiment, a laboratory for discovering the impact of different approaches to small groups. They identified their most likely suspects for small-group leaders, and each agreed to recruit two.

At the next weekly tactical meeting, the news was that *only one* of their eight potential recruits said yes. They spent the next hour strategizing how to better their chances of recruiting seven more leaders. Again they identified their likely suspects. But this time, they made their recruiting calls before they left the meeting.

And so the process went. With a rhythm of periodic strategic meetings and weekly tactical meetings, Lesleigh's small-group launch team attempted, failed, revised plans, failed again and made incremental progress after incremental progress.

At the end of the year, they all agreed they'd made progress, but the small-group program was clearly not yet sustainable. When Lesleigh gave her team an "out," none of them chose to step aside, each acknowledging that, without even trying, they'd actually lived a profound small-group experience together. They agreed to add two more members and to continue working their weekly assignments until the youth ministry's small-group program had grown into the description they had crafted at the beginning of the process.

It took three years. But by that time, their incremental progress had almost imperceptibly resulted in exponential change. Not only was the small-group ministry thriving, but the church was using Lesleigh's structure as a model for revamping their approach to the adult small-group ministry.

With a combination of persistence and intentionality, Lesleigh's team had created a steady drumbeat that eventually transformed its most floundering program into its most effective one. Consider the differences between Lesleigh's process and the "normal" way a youth worker might address a small-group problem (see table 1).

Persons with comparatively moderate powers will accomplish much if they apply themselves wholly and indefatigably to one thing at a time.

SAMUEL SMILES

In Rosabeth Moss Kanter's study of winning and losing streaks, she found three consistent components in winning organizations: accountability, collaboration and initiative. When these three strategic bedrocks become standard operating procedure for a team (as they did for Lesleigh's), scaling brick walls simply becomes a normal way that ministry responds to challenges.

Table 1.

Sustainable Approach	Traditional Approach
Long-term focus on a single issue	Episodic focus with key issue buried beneath multiple issues in disconnected meetings
Responsibility shared by a team	Responsibility carried by the youth worker
Regular meetings	Concerns raised reactively and urgently at random meetings
Regular time set aside for strategic thinking	Issue addressed between the urgent demands of the ministry
The expectation of a multiyear building process	The expectation of the quick fix
Working a plan	Reacting to anxiousness

Lesleigh's small-group team not only became experts in understanding small groups; they also became experts in implementing a powerful collaborative process, the very process they would implement over and over in the years to come, as they dealt with the brick walls of curriculum, attendance and worship.

If Lesleigh's process felt tedious to you, if you got impatient reading it, welcome to the club. The brick walls of youth ministry will not be scaled using the next great idea. Strategic plans are not enough. It's working those plans in a strategic way (and getting back up again and again when the initial plans fail) that ultimately makes the difference.

IMMERSED IN THE (RIGHT) DETAILS

If there is one refrain I hear more than any other from frustrated youth workers, it's "I just get mired in the details." I have to admit that I've aired that complaint more than once myself. But then I talked to Scott.

Scott is a dear brother in my church, the chairman of our youth committee and one of the most successful, effective leaders I've ever known—in his home, in his business, in our church. I once asked him what sets his businesses apart, why they've been so successful.

I was, at first, taken aback by his response: "We get into the details. Most companies that do what we do give advice," he said. "They tell people what to do. We get into the details of a company's problems . . . and we solve them."

One of the keys to an effective youth ministry is that someone with enough experience to tell the gold from the coal is "getting into the details." Throughout the last thirteen chapters, we've worked with building images—architects, construction, foundations—on purpose. Sustainable youth ministries—built to withstand pressures from outside the church and politics from within—are established when a construction team has learned to pay attention to *the right details*.

EPILOGUE

Seizing the Unfair Advantage

When you want something, all the universe conspires in helping you achieve it.

PAULO COELHO

Make everything as simple as possible, but not simpler.

ALBERT EINSTEIN

I often think my most valuable credential is my vast repertoire of stupid mistakes through the years, mistakes that can't help but teach their perpetrator something the hard way.

BRIAN McLAREN

I learned about unfair advantages during Adam's senior year, at his regional cross-country meet.

The regional meet is the one that determines which runners qualify for state. For a high-school senior, this is undoubtedly the most important meet of his or her high-school career. Run well, you run again with even higher stakes the next week. Run poorly, and your cross-country career is over.

As always, the team's mood just before the race was intense—not a lot of talking or joking, clearly a team with its game face on. The mood was so pervasive, it even subdued us fans. But once the race began, all our reserve flew out the window. We screamed and shouted encouragement to any one of our runners within earshot, running back and forth across the course, strategically placing ourselves so we could cheer our boy and his team five or six times before they crossed the finish line.

Adam's team did well, winning the regional meet, as I recall. We pushed our way through the crowd of runners to meet up with Adam at the end of the race, handed him a Gatorade and hugged our stinky, sweaty runner. For the next twenty or thirty minutes, we celebrated him and his team. As we wandered the course with him, he introduced us to friends from other schools, one of whom gave me a picture of youth ministry I'll never forget.

After Adam introduced us to an attractive young woman, a senior he'd met at a Fellowship of Christian Athletes camp, he asked her, "So how did you do?" She smiled, raised her eyebrows and said, "Well, my *time* qualified me for state."

Adam responded immediately, "That's incredible! Congratulations!" But while the words were still in his mouth, she completed her sentence:

"But . . . I was disqualified."

We were dumbfounded. How in the world, we asked, was she disqualified?

She explained that in the last few hundred yards of the race, one of her teammates, an enthusiastic young man, was cheering her on from the sidelines, running alongside her and screaming words of encouragement as she pushed her way up the final hill to the finish line.

Adam and I responded in unison, "So?"

"It turns out," she said, "that having a pacer running alongside you gives you an unfair advantage. They had to disqualify me."

The referees were right. It's true in running, and it's true in youth ministry. Having a pace runner gives an undeniable advantage. So, if you're finishing this book and asking, "Now what?" one of the first steps is to seize the unfair advantage of finding a youth ministry pacer.

Whether you're a senior pastor, a youth pastor or a volunteer stakeholder in your church's youth ministry, your church will periodically need pacers who can play at least three roles for you: referee, coach and commissioner.

Sometimes a church can find pacers close at hand, either inside or outside the church. At other times, particularly when a youth ministry is at a critical juncture, the church may choose to "outsource" these responsibilities to those with expertise in playing these roles. A church's first step is to recognize that these three roles will, at times, be absolutely necessary for sustaining a thriving youth ministry.

THE REFEREE (FOR THE SYSTEM)

Everyone at St. Paul's Church was well intentioned. The pastor talked to the associate pastor who talked to the youth director who talked to the interns. Everyone talked to the volunteers, who were left confused by the mixed messages they received. Every now and then the pastor would parachute in, rifle off advice from his own experience in youth ministry (twenty years prior), scowl a bit and retreat to the relative safety of an elders meeting.

Everyone in this system *wanted* to do the right thing. But they were mired in anxiousness, with competing visions and patterns of management that were counterproductive at best. We knew we had to get all the players around the same table. But revising the organizational chart for the ministry and having a meeting or two would simply not be enough.

This ministry needed someone who could bring the group back together when (not if) someone on the team was "playing" in a way contrary to the agreed-upon strategic plan. Having a referee didn't mean that the rules couldn't change. It simply meant that a change in direction was agreed on and communicated with clarity to the entire team.

Over a period of months, clarity slowly began to emerge. Confusion and mixed messages disappeared almost entirely, and the team began to reengage *together* in a clear, strategic work to which they had all been called.

Every now and then, Youth Ministry Architects invites a "systems referee" into *our* organization to raise questions and diagnose our weak spots. I remember one of those meetings with painful clarity. Our referee asked us seemingly simple questions about our organization, questions like "What is it that you do?" For an hour, he pummeled our team with enough questions to narrow our focus from a vague blur to a laser-point focus on what we were called to do together.

Because he was positioned outside the system, he could see things and raise questions that were simply outside the imagination of those of us doing the work.

With all-too-common short-sightedness, most churches want their youth ministries to grow, but few have a system in place to ensure that, as their ministry grows, its foundation expands to hold the additional weight. Making sure this essential expansion happens in the appropriate sequence is part of the work of a systems referee.

> **First, it is reasonable to expect the insiders of any bureaucratic system will defend that institution and its past actions. Second, it is unreasonable to expect those same insiders to be able and willing to conduct a comprehensive and critical analysis of any systems failure in the institution. Third, it is rarely possible to "fix the current system" without challenging and changing the institutional culture.**
>
> LYLE SCHALLER

THE COACH (FOR THE YOUTH STAFF)

In the first months of ministry, it's far too easy for a new youth worker to breathe in the numbing gas of congratulations ("You *are* the Pied Piper!") and the quiet whispers of validation ("You're so much better than that last person who was here"). Unaware of how often these effusive affirmations are coming from people who desperately want to believe they've hired the right person, the inexperienced youth worker settles into an easy complacency, as if he or she has little left to learn.

But it's at this point that the new youth worker is most in danger—in danger of creating a ministry in which he or she is the center, in danger of building on a foundation of sand, in danger of settling into a lone-ranger mentality that's almost the opposite of what's needed for sustainability.

In one of the classic *I Love Lucy* episodes, Ricky finds Lucy on all fours in the living room, obviously searching for something. When he asks what she's doing, she explains that she's looking for her lost earrings.

He asks, "You lost your earrings in the living room?"

"No, I lost them in the bedroom—but the light is so much better out here."

It's natural for youth workers to look for solutions in the easy spots, the spots where "the light is so much better." But if youth workers are going to leverage their efforts to move their youth ministry forward, they'll need the encouragement and accountability to look for answers in places that may, at times, be outside their own comfort zones.

In an average month, I'll spend a few hours picking the brains of experts—experts in ministry, in business, in leadership, in parenting, in marriage, even those I perceive as "experts" at following Christ. For me, the words of Woodrow Wilson make sense: "I not only use all the brains I have, but all the brains I can borrow."

Without a coach, a youth ministry is reduced to the size of the leader's comfort zone. We all need people who are honest enough to help us move from making excuses to making progress.

This is not to say that many youth directors don't produce immediate results. But too many "thriving" youth groups keep growing faster and faster until they self-destruct of their own momentum. With everyone infatuated with immediate growth, it's easy to ignore the need to lay a sustainable foundation—until the exhausted youth worker spins out of control and resigns.

A COMMISSIONER (FOR THE TRANSITIONS)

Most churches need—and need desperately—the one thing they don't think they can afford: someone with years of experience, someone who isn't going anywhere, someone who can provide continuity through the inevitable chaos of youth leaders and volunteers coming and going, someone who can come alongside the church to help hold the wheel through the turbulent waters of transition, someone old enough and connected enough to provide the weight to keep the ship righted when winds are wild and the waves are high.

I'm not talking about a permanent superstar youth director (that mythical kind that never dies and never ages). I'm talking about a permanent *relationship* with a commissioner, an ongoing connection with an organization that understands both the church and the "sustainability game" in youth ministry, who can assist with an annual audit to ensure that all the foundational systems are in place and well maintained. Some churches may find this kind of support in their denominational office, while others may choose to contact an independent consulting group. (For options related to finding a commissioner organization, visit www .ymarchitects.com.)

JUST ASK WAIN

Wain was under fire when I first got his call. His youth leaders were rebelling, reacting, doing anything but following his lead. Anxiousness, perhaps the most contagious of all ecclesial diseases, had drawn Wain into reacting to the negativity and defensiveness around him. And it wasn't working.

In many ways, the criticism leveled at Wain was far from fair. When he invited Youth Ministry Architects into the process, though, we determined together to focus less on the content of the criticism and more on doing the kinds of things we've outlined in the last thirteen chapters.

Wain was a quick learner, taking initiative and following through consistently on the recommendations he received. And slowly, over the next year and a half, the youth ministry made the shift. As it moved to more solid footing, Wain did as well, moving from anxiousness and defensiveness ("It's not in my job description") to being a catalytic leader ("Let's figure it out together!").

No longer a victim of unrealistic expectations, Wain soon found the margin to take on increasing responsibility in his church, often becoming the go-to guy on staff when a new initiative was being launched. No longer crushed by the pyramid of expectations on top of him, he was now on top of that pyramid—leading his teams, managing the infrastructure, bringing new and creative programs to the table. As he began hitting the benchmarks agreed on by the church leadership, the unfair criticism and submarine attacks dropped almost completely out of sight.

If you ask Wain's wife, she'll tell you that the shift in her husband's ministry had a collateral effect on the climate of their home. Wain's family time became more predictable, providing enough margin to yield a relaxed response from his bride when a ministerial emergency or unexpected late-night meeting came up.

Though some see asking for support as a sign of weakness, our experience has been that the exact opposite is true. Those bold enough to ask for support early enough in the process dramatically increase their chances of persevering through the demands of long-term youth ministry. Sustained youth ministers almost always produce sustainable youth ministries (and vice versa).

> **What is your only hope in life and death?**
>
> That I belong—body and soul, in life and in death—not to myself but to my faithful Savior, Jesus Christ, who at the cost of his own blood has fully paid for all my sins and has completely freed me from the dominion of the devil; that he protects me so well that without the will of my Father in heaven not a hair can fall from my head; indeed, that everything must fit his purpose for my salvation. Therefore by his Holy Spirit he also assures me of eternal life and makes me wholeheartedly willing and ready from now on to live for him.
>
> HEIDELBERG CATECHISM, QUESTION 1

TAKING THE LONG VIEW

Sue Monk Kidd's words about the transformation of the heart are equally true about the transformation of an organization: "New life comes slowly, awkwardly, on wobbly wings." I've watched it happen in our own ministry, where I've been a poster child for Winston Churchill's curious definition of success: "One failure after another . . . with enthusiasm!"

Whether you're starting from scratch, renovating an established youth ministry or hoping to breathe new life into a place that has been stuck for years, remember as you begin that "everything can look like a failure in the middle." And whether you're a "lifer" who plans to work with teenagers until your dying breath or someone who plans to provide support from a distance, I invite you to join in the chorus calling the church back to investing in a generation of young disciples who can transform their homes, their schools, their churches, their workplaces and their world for Christ.

Youth ministry is a high and holy calling. But we must never be confused: youth ministry is not the hope of the world. The next generation of disciples is not the hope of the world. Our faith tells us clearly that Jesus Christ alone is the hope of the world.

Sustainable youth ministries seek to steward the true Treasure in faithful jars of clay, knowing full well that these vessels of structure and strategy, of leadership and leverage, are only temporary, though necessary, means of bearing the gospel to the next generation.

Carry on.

APPENDIX A

Introduction: A Roll of the Dice

1. As you read through *Sustainable Youth Ministry*, who are the others on your team you would like to share the conversation with?

2. When has your youth ministry taken a gambler's approach to building a thriving youth ministry?

Chapter 1: Cracking the Code

1. Look back at the story of your youth ministry over the past ten years. What patterns bubble up?

2. Which of the characteristics of a stuck youth ministry have you seen in your own context?

Chapter 2: The Easy Button

1. Which of the youth ministry normals fit or don't fit your particular ministry?

2. Do the math for your ministry to determine the current baseline capacity of your youth ministry, given the rules of thumb identified in this chapter.

3. What are the biggest obstacles to your church investing at a level that matches its expectations for youth ministry?

Chapter 3: Hoping, Wishing and Praying

1. Review the traits of a church with a superstar mentality and consider which, if any, apply to your church or ministry.

2. How would the leaders of your church respond to the notion of "hiring from within"?

3. Look at the history of your youth staff. Which previous youth staff members stepped into thriving ministries after leaving your church? Who has been sidelined from ministry altogether?

Chapter 4: The Dance Floor

1. After this brief introduction to systems thinking, what questions do you have?

2. Would you say your ministry is more systems focused, or staff or program focused? In what ways?

Chapter 5: Building Right

1. Which of the control documents does your ministry have in place?

2. Which of the visioning documents does your ministry have in place?

3. What prevents your ministry from "squaring the corners" and getting the key structures outlined in this chapter in place?

4. If you had to guess, what is the target number of youth the leaders of your church would like to see involved on an average week?

5. What would a group look like that was perfectly structured to create cliques? That was perfectly structured to create apathy in students? That was perfectly structured for eleventh- and twelfth-graders to drop out?

Chapter 6: Changing Culture

1. If you were to give a weather report of the climate of your current youth ministry, what would that report be?

2. What stories and metaphors define the culture of your youth ministry?

   • a story of a time when "God showed up" in your youth ministry

   • a story of unexpected grace in your youth ministry

   • a story of a student's unlikely connection to your church

Chapter 7: Searching Right

1. What worked well in your church's last search for youth staff?

2. If your current youth worker were to resign today, how ready is your church to engage in an effective search and to walk through the transition without losing momentum?

3. In what ways will your next search process have to "start from scratch" and in what ways will it rely on processes developed in previous searches?

4. On your current youth ministry team, who plays the role of the architect? The general contractor? The craftsperson?

Chapter 8: Aligning the Heart

1. What are the warning signs that a youth staff person is not doing ministry from an emotionally healthy place?

2. What are the unique stressors on your youth staff as they seek to do youth ministry from an emotionally healthy place?

3. Who can provide support and accountability for the youth staff to maximize the chances of tending to their own souls and not simply to their ministries?

4. Why do some youth workers consider it selfish to set personal boundaries?

5. How would you counsel a youth minister who loves kids so much that he or she is consistently sacrificing his or her own emotional health to do the job?

Chapter 9: Monkeys, Frogs and Balconies

1. How would the leaders of your church respond to a youth staff person taking two to three hours of balcony time away from the office each week?

2. How would you rate your current youth staff's ability to eat frogs and manage ministry monkeys?

Chapter 10: Architecting the Constellation

1. How can your church be more effective in creating a constellation of relationships for each of the youth in your ministry?

2. What are the biggest challenges your ministry faces in developing a team of volunteers to serve in the youth ministry?

3. Who "owns the monkey" of recruiting in your ministry?

Chapter 11: The Magnet Effect

1. If you were to guess, how comfortable would you say that first-timers are in your youth ministry?

2. How often do visiting youth become active participants in your ministry?

3. How often in the previous year have you asked visitors for their impressions of the youth ministry, using questions like these:

- Overall, how did your experience with our group meet your expectations? Where there any parts that exceeded your expectations? Any that fell below your expectations?

- How likely are you to recommend our group to someone else? Are you very likely . . . very unlikely?

- How likely are you to want to return to participate in our group again? Are you very likely . . . very unlikely?

4. Which youth in your ministry are the ones most likely to take responsibility for creating a welcoming culture?

5. Og Mandino argued that "the only certain means of success is to render more and better service than is expected of you, no matter what your task may be."

- Does this principle hold true for ministry?

- How would Jesus respond to this statement?

- Based on this statement, was Jesus successful?

Chapter 12: Dancing with Alligators

1. What are some of the unspoken rules for how decisions are made in your church?

2. How much "political capital" would you say the current youth ministry has in the larger church?

3. What are some of the surest ways of building "political capital" for the youth ministry?

4. What are the most important expectations your senior pastor has for the youth ministry of your church?

Chapter 13: Rabbit Trails and Brick Walls

1. What are some of the more tempting rabbit trails that might pull your youth ministry off course?

2. What brick walls has your youth ministry run into?

Epilogue: Seizing the Unfair Advantage

1. After having read through the processes of building a sustainable youth ministry, what are the first steps your ministry needs to take?

2. What additional resources—both inside and outside the church—will you need in order to accomplish your church's dreams for its youth ministry?

APPENDIX B

Sustainable Youth Ministry Builder's List

Though the building of every church's youth ministry is unique, some foundational steps must be taken in almost every church to make its youth ministry sustainable. The Sustainable Youth Ministry Builder's List is a starting point, a diagnostic tool that can serve as an accessible outline of the first steps in building a youth ministry that lasts.

STAGE 1: CREATING THE BLUEPRINT, PREPARING FOR THE PROCESS

Control Documents

❑ Youth directory

❑ Twelve-month major event calendar

❑ Recruiting needs list (partners)

- Sunday mornings

    Number of different settings:
    Number of volunteers needed:

- Small groups

    Number of groups:
    Number of volunteers needed:

- Large group(s)

    Number of different settings:
    Number of volunteers needed:

- Major-event coordinators

    Number of volunteers needed:

❑ Recruiting pool list
    Names: (behind the scenes, with kids, or both)
    Rating: (A, B, C)

❑ Job descriptions

Visioning Documents

❑ Mission statement

❑ Values

❑ Three-year revolving goals / one-year benchmarks

❑ Organizational chart: Including who will play the role of the architect, the general contractor and the craftspeople

STAGE 2: LAYING THE FOUNDATION

❑ Recruiting a partner volunteer team

❑ Gaining buy-in/approval for the visioning documents from key stakeholders, including the senior pastor, elders and so on

❑ Contacting every student in the youth ministry

❑ Learning the names of every student in the youth ministry

❑ Contacting every parent of youth in the youth ministry

❑ Selecting a "good enough" curriculum for the rest of the year

❑ Developing a youth ministry communication plan.

STAGE 3: BEGINNING TO BUILD

❑ Scheduling regular volunteer leader gatherings

❑ One-on-one or one-on-two face-to-face meetings with all volunteers

❑ Long-term staffing plan (to provide capacity to achieve the three-year goals)

❑ Developing a recruiting needs list (helpers)

- Communications coordinator

    Web
    Bulletin board
    Church publications

- Food coordinator

❑ Youth ministry manual

❑ Curriculum template (six- or seven-year plan)

❑ Compliance documents: music and video copyright licensing, background checks, child protection policy

❑ Major-event notebooks

STAGE 4: FRAMING THE SECOND FLOOR

❑ Student apprenticeship process

❑ Parent engagement events

❑ Game plan for integrating youth into the life of the larger church

❑ Executing one high-impact/high-visibility program

❑ Developing a game plan for launching small groups

❑ Updating youth ministry facilities

APPENDIX C

The Compliance Checklist

____ Do we do background checks on the volunteers who work on a hands-on basis in our youth ministry?

____ Does your church have supplemental auto liability coverage that kicks in after a youth trip driver's individual coverage has been exhausted?

____ Do you have an up-to-date Church Copyright License for music and an up-to-date Church Video License for videos used in the youth ministry?

____ Do you have a clear policy about students driving students and about drivers under twenty-five driving students?

____ Do you have a policy that bars new members working in the youth ministry until a waiting period of six months has been completed?

____ Do you have in writing a brief summary from your church's insurance agent about what is and is not covered when you are taking a trip away from the church?

____ Do you have the phone number to call if you are involved in an accident on a church trip?

___ Do you have a resource like Church Risk Management readily at hand?

___ Do you ask for written applications from every volunteer?

___ Do you (or someone on your team) interview every prospective volunteer?

ACKNOWLEDGMENTS

I'm not all that original; I just seem to be able to get the tune out of my head and onto my lips a little before others do. When I hum it, others often say, "That tune was in my mind already, but I just couldn't access it."
BRIAN McLAREN

This book is a culmination of countless conversations with partners in ministry who have been bold enough to join in this adventure of failing forward. This book would have been undeniably less without the influence, support and loyal opposition of a wide assortment of companions on the journey:

The dream team youth staff at First Presbyterian Church of Nashville (B. J., Ellie, Erika, Linda, Mary Lee, Matt, Trey and Becky), who know the reality of trying to build a sustainable youth ministry and how often we fall short of our own dreams.

The youth and adult leaders of FPC who have, again and again, surprised us with the ways that they have embraced a deeper, richer, more honest journey with Christ than any of our great ideas could have ever produced.

Tom and Lisa's Youth Leader Parent group, who dedicated months to reading, reviewing and giving the kind of input that has hopefully made these pages just a little more useful to the people who need them most.

The curious cohort of holy friends on our Youth Ministry Architects lead staff (Jeff, Colyer, Lesleigh, Jen, Lynn, Sara, Dave, Jack and Marie), who lived the principles of this book years before we had time to put them in writing. We all know that for everything in these pages that works, there were countless half-baked ideas that, thanks to you, never made it out of the laboratory.

Our growing family of YMA churches, who have entrusted us with the awesome privilege of mentoring, befriending and partnering in this journey of building sustainable youth ministries one church at a time.

The team at the Center for Youth Ministry Training (Deech, Keeley, Will, Lesleigh, the CYMT board of directors and the Lilly Foundation), for their relentless commitment to dream big dreams for the future of youth ministry and for the bridges they are building between the academy and those of us who find ourselves working with youth every day.

My own great cloud of witnesses, including

- my pastor, Todd Jones, and the elders and staff of First Presbyterian Church, who grant me much more freedom and honor than I deserve

- Rick, Doug, Andy, and the folks at Group, Simply and youthministry .com

- Kenda, Amy, Dayle, Kendy, Emily, Pat and all the folks in the Institute for Youth Ministry at Princeton Theological Seminary, who have provided a forum for turning vague, fragmented ideas into systemic ways of conceptualizing youth ministry

- Jim, Wayne, Mary and our friends at Homeword

- Chan Sheppard, my running buddy and number one counselor who solidifies my thinking and listens deeply through my labored breathing, and his wife, Ginger, who has a way of turning my chaos into order

- Anne, Kristen, David, Ian and Julian, for your role in YMA's incremental revolution

- George and Trish, Kirk and Debbie, Chuck and Penny, Craig and Sherri, Karl, Scott and Elaine, Andy and Sue, Dan, Steve and Mary Lee, Billy and Cathryn, Robert and Bobbie, Mark and Kate, Mom, Dad, Louise, Gene and Bernice, John and Delia, Rick, the Mat Friends, and the Nashville Youth Ministry Geezers

- My faithful and forgiving editor, Cindy Bunch, who always has a way of making me sound better than I ever could have without her.

- Adam, Sara, Debbie and Leigh, who have long since moved from being our children to being our dearest friends and partners in the gospel.

- My bride, Susan. You're right. No man ever had it so good.

And to the God who has a way of working best through those broken enough to allow the light of Christ to shine through the cracks.

NOTES

Introduction: A Roll of the Dice

page 13   "a senior pastor who understands and loves teenagers": Rick Lawrence, "The Cool Church," *Group Magazine,* May 6, 2001, p. 37.

Chapter 1: Cracking the Code

page 24   "the size of a congregation's youth group is the greatest predictor": Merton Strommen, Karen E. Jones and Dave Rahn, *Youth Ministry That Transforms: A Comprehensive Analysis of the Hopes, Frustrations, and Effectiveness of Today's Youth Workers* (Grand Rapids: Zondervan, 2001), p. 268.

page 24   "Youth go where the numbers are": Jim Burns and Mike DeVries, *The Youth Builder: Today's Resource for Relational Youth Ministry* (Ventura, Calif.: Gospel Light, 2001), chap. 1.

page 27   But when probed further about what was meant: John Maxwell, *Failing Forward: Turning Mistakes into Stepping-Stones for Success* (Nashville: Thomas Nelson, 2000), p. 155.

Chapter 2: The Easy Button

pages 29-30 most crippling myths about youth ministry: I first introduced the concept of the Easy Button in youth ministry in Mark DeVries, "The Easy Button," *Group Magazine,* May-June 2006, p. 42.

page 31   "More than half of adolescents who attend church": Kenda Creasy Dean, *Practicing Passion: Youth and the Quest for a Passionate Church* (Grand Rapids: Eerdmans, 2004), p. 147.

page 32   In one longitudinal study, 48 percent of adults: Dean R. Hoge, Benton Johnson and Donald A. Luidens, *Vanishing Boundaries: The Religion of Mainline Baby Boomers* (Louisville: Westminster/John Knox, 1994), p. 68.

page 32   "More than seven out of ten teens are engaged in some church-related":

Barna Research Group, *Third Millennium Teens,* quoted in Ben Burns, "Helping Seniors Finish Strong," *Network Magazine,* March 2003, p. 3.

page 32   "In a typical week, just three out of 10 twentysomethings": Kristen Campbell, "Youth Aren't Finding What They Need in Church," *Jackson (Tennessee) Sun,* December 27, 2003, p. 2C.

page 32   From high school graduation to age 25: "Barna, 2003," quoted in Student Life Bible study advertisement, *Group Magazine,* July-August 2006.

page 32   "We're debating about whether to have carpet": Louie Giglio, general session #6 address, National Youth Workers Convention, Nashville, November 17-21, 2005.

page 37   at around 10 percent of the worshiping congregation: Len Kageler affirms this ratio in his *How to Expand Your Youth Ministry* (Grand Rapids: Zondervan, 1996), p. 14.

Chapter 3: Hoping, Wishing and Praying

page 45   "We delegate youth ministry to folks who are": Ted Smith, plenary session, Princeton Forum on Youth Ministry, January 7-10, 2007.

page 47   the CEO was *not* a superstar savior: Jim Collins, *Good to Great* (New York: HarperBusiness, 2001).

page 48   "Of the various ministry positions, youth ministers": Merton Strommen, Karen E. Jones and Dave Rahn, *Youth Ministry That Transforms: A Comprehensive Analysis of the Hopes, Frustrations, and Effectiveness of Today's Youth Workers* (Grand Rapids: Zondervan, 2001), pp. 34-35.

Chapter 5: Building Right

page 65   By allowing multiple groups to work on drafting: Patrick Lencioni, *The Five Temptations of a CEO: A Leadership Fable* (San Francisco: Jossey-Bass, 1998), p. 127.

page 65   More important than education, family background, intelligence: From Edward Banfield, *The Unheavenly City,* quoted in Brian Tracy, *Eat That Frog! 21 Great Ways to Stop Procrastinating and Get More Done in Less Time* (San Francisco: Berrett-Koehler Publishers, 2007), p. 25.

page 66   "a sort of Christian 'club' that [exhausts] itself": Robert Lewis, *The Church of Irresistible Influence* (Grand Rapids: Eerdmans, 2001), p. 29.

page 72   "what got them big in the first place": Thomas J. Peters and Robert H. Waterman, *In Search of Excellence* (New York: HarperBusiness Essentials, 2004), p. 200, emphasis mine.

page 72   The National Science Foundation discovered: Doug Fields, *Your First Two Years in Youth Ministry* (El Cajon, Calif.: Youth Specialties, 2002), p. 227.

Chapter 6: Changing Culture

page 85   The laughing groups were consistently better at solving: Retold in Thom and Joani Schultz, *The Dirt on Learning* (Loveland, Colo.: Group, 1999), pp. 166-67.

page 87   Children—and churches—tend to live into the words: Jeanne Mayo, *Thriving Youth Groups: Secrets for Growing Your Ministry* (Loveland, Colo.: Group, 2005), p. 78.

Chapter 7: Searching Right

page 92   The average youth minister serves: "The 18-Month Myth is now part of
              youth ministry lore. It's been used over and over to describe youth minis-
              ters as easily scared gypsies who bolt at the first sign of trouble. And it's all
              a bunch of bunk. We . . . asked our research staff to complete a scientific
              survey of North American churches using a representative sampling of
              denominations. We discovered that the average paid youth minister has
              been at the same church for almost four years (3.9 years, to be exact)"
              (Rick Lawrence, "3 Dirty, Rotten Youth Ministry Lies," *Group Magazine*,
              September-October 2006, p. 77).

page 95   "I've heard too many horror stories": Doug Fields, *Your First Two Years in
              Youth Ministry* (El Cajon, Calif.: Youth Specialties, 2002), p. 257.

page 95   "Get the right person in the right job": Tom Paterson, *Living the Life You
              Were Meant to Live* (Nashville: Thomas Nelson, 1998), p. 205.

page 100   By some estimates, a bad church hire: Mike Woodruff, *Managing Youth
              Ministry Chaos* (Loveland, Colo.: Group, 2000), p. 43.

page 101   The research he shared shows: From a conversation with Dean Trulear in
              Seattle in January 2005.

page 102   He goes on to give a surprising description: Michael Gerber, *The E-Myth
              Revisited* (New York: HarperBusiness, 1995), p. 181.

pages 102-3 When Doug Fields asked parents in his church: Fields, *First Two Years*, p. 261.

page 103   A decade or so ago, the average full-time youth worker's: Merton Strom-
              men, Karen E. Jones and Dave Rahn, *Youth Ministry That Transforms: A
              Comprehensive Analysis of the Hopes, Frustrations, and Effectiveness of To-
              day's Youth Workers* (Grand Rapids: Zondervan, 2001), p. 73.

page 103   Figure 6: Posted at <http://www.payscale.com/research/US/Job=Youth
              Pastor/Salary/by_Years_Experience>. Accessed September 5, 2008.

page 104   In addition to salary, a church will want to consider: Strommen, Jones and
              Rahn, *Youth Ministry*, p. 74, offers 1999 statistics on how common such
              benefits are for youth workers.

Chapter 8: Aligning the Heart

page 109   "The overall health of any church or ministry": Peter Scazzero, *The Emo-
              tionally Healthy Church: A Strategy for Discipleship That Actually Changes
              Lives* (Grand Rapids: Zondervan, 2003), p. 1.

page 110   On one list of concerns of professional youth ministers: Merton Strommen,
              Karen E. Jones and Dave Rahn, *Youth Ministry That Transforms: A Compre-
              hensive Analysis of the Hopes, Frustrations, and Effectiveness of Today's Youth
              Workers* (Grand Rapids: Zondervan, 2001), pp. 20-21.

page 112   "The 'dream' is rarely realized": Michael Gerber, *The E-Myth Revisited* (New
              York: HarperBusiness, 1995), p. 263.

page 112   She suggests that our wounds have a way: Sue Monk Kidd, *When the Heart
              Waits: Spiritual Direction for Life's Sacred Questions* (San Francisco: Harper
              & Row, 1990), p. 155.

page 114   Center for Youth Ministry Training: Visit their website at <www.cymt
              .org.>

page 115   The research also discovered that "high aptitude in arts": Erwin McManus,
              An Unstoppable Force: Daring to Become the Church God Had in Mind (Love-

land, Colo.: Group, 2001), pp. 128-29, including a quote from Robert Root-Bernstein, professor of physiology at Michigan State University, in an article called "Hobbled Arts Limit Our Future."

page 117   Jim Collins suggests: Jerry Useem, "Jim Collins on Tough Calls," *Fortune*, June 27, 2005.

page 120   "The person who hurts the most": John Maxwell, *Winning with People* (Nashville: Nelson Business, 2004), audio book, disk 1.

page 120   "I've known many 'cool' youth leaders": Jeanne Mayo, *Thriving Youth Groups: Secrets for Growing Your Ministry* (Loveland, Colo.: Group, 2005), p. 102.

page 123   The wick begins to burn only when the oil: Adapted from Richard R. Dunn, *Shaping the Spiritual Life of Students* (Downers Grove, Ill.: InterVarsity Press, 2001), pp. 227-28.

Chapter 9: Monkeys, Frogs and Balconies

pages 125-26 "No church in America has sustained a large youth ministry": Ron King, "Super Glue," *NNYM Magazine*, December 2002, p. 7.

page 126   In addition, both the level of satisfaction: Merton Strommen, Karen E. Jones and Dave Rahn, *Youth Ministry That Transforms: A Comprehensive Analysis of the Hopes, Frustrations, and Effectiveness of Today's Youth Workers* (Grand Rapids: Zondervan, 2001), p. 235.

page 126   "Persevere. The longer you minister with youth": Strommen, Jones and Rahn, *Youth Ministry*, p. 238.

page 126   "My daughter—an active member of the youth group": "Ask & Receive," *Group Magazine*, July-August 2006, p. 30.

page 127   And conflict turns out to be, far and away, the number-one reason: King, "Super Glue," p. 7.

pages 129-30 It's About Time: Some of the ideas in this section of chapter nine first appeared in Mark DeVries, "The Hunt for Buried Treasure: Time Management for A.D.D. Youth Workers," *Group Magazine*.

pages 131-33 Balcony Time: Some of the ideas about balcony time were first introduced in the following article: Mark DeVries, "The Need for Balcony Time: Why Most Youth Ministries Never Get Off the Dime," *Group Magazine*, May-June 2004.

page 132   A Sabbath is a day off from work: Paraphrase from Doug Fields, *Your First Two Years in Youth Ministry* (El Cajon, Calif.: Youth Specialties, 2002), p. 57.

page 133   Where Have All Your Monkeys Gone?: The monkey management principles first appeared in a series of articles in *Group Magazine*, inspired by Ken Blanchard, William Oncken Jr. and Hal Burrows's *The One-Minute Manager Meets the Monkey* (New York: Morrow, 1989).

Chapter 10: Architecting the Constellation

page 145   "This was the first year that I ever felt included": Jeanne Mayo, *Thriving Youth Groups: Secrets for Growing Your Ministry* (Loveland, Colo.: Group, 2005), p. 93.

page 145   The study behind the book *Youth Ministry That Transforms*: Merton Strommen, Karen E. Jones and Dave Rahn, *Youth Ministry That Transforms: A Comprehensive Analysis of the Hopes, Frustrations, and Effectiveness of To-*

day's Youth Workers (Grand Rapids: Zondervan, 2001), p. 206.

page 152   He calls us "stewards of a community of dreamers": Erwin McManus, *An Unstoppable Force: Daring to Become the Church God Had in Mind* (Loveland, Colo.: Group, 2001), p. 196.

page 153   But less than 25 percent of that same group: Strommen, Jones and Rahn, *Youth Ministry*, p. 220. An interesting sidebar for my own denomination: we Presbyterians came in dead last in developing volunteers, with our cousins the Lutherans and the Episcopalians only a few steps ahead of us.

page 155   But that number jumps significantly for the seniors: Mike Nappa, *What I Wish My Youth Leader Knew About Youth Ministry: A National Survey* (Cincinnati: Standard, 1999), p. 183.

page 156   Calvin revises his statement, "I thrive on making": John Maxwell, *Failing Forward: Turning Mistakes into Stepping-Stones for Success* (Nashville: Thomas Nelson, 2000), p. 160.

page 156   "the losing companies are twice as likely": Rosabeth Moss Kanter, *Confidence: How Winning Streaks and Losing Streaks Begin and End* (New York: Crown Business, 2004), p. 99.

Chapter 11: The Magnet Effect

page 161   Interestingly, the third-highest response: Rick Lawrence, "The Cool Church," *Group Magazine*, May 6, 2001, p. 37.

pages 164-65 In *Practicing Passion*, Kenda Dean identifies: Kenda Creasy Dean, *Practicing Passion: Youth and the Quest for a Passionate Church* (Grand Rapids: Eerdmans, 2004), pp. 73-144.

page 165   Some experts suggest that unless a newcomer: Len Kageler, *How to Expand Your Youth Ministry* (Grand Rapids: Zondervan, 1996), p. 41.

page 165   "When I was a sophomore in high school": Jeanne Mayo, *Thriving Youth Groups: Secrets for Growing Your Ministry* (Loveland, Colo.: Group, 2005), p. 69.

page 168   "So why did I ask you to show up tonight?": Mayo, *Thriving*, p. 28.

page 168   One church asks their friendship-epidemic students: "Most Wanted List" idea borrowed from Kageler, *How to Expand*, p. 25.

page 170   "We all come from different backgrounds": Mayo, *Thriving*, p. 76.

page 172   "student movements led by students below the college": Mark Senter, *The Coming Revolution in Youth Ministry* (Wheaton Ill.: Victor, 1992), p. 52.

Chapter 12: Dancing with Alligators

pages 176-77 "Most careers involve other people": Quoted in John Maxwell, *Failing Forward: Turning Mistakes into Stepping-Stones for Success* (Nashville: Thomas Nelson, 2000), p. 155.

page 177   In a study of 185 youth pastors who'd been fired: Len Kageler, *How to Expand Your Youth Ministry* (Grand Rapids: Zondervan, 1996), p. 21.

page 179   The porcupine party: Concept borrowed from John Maxwell, *Winning with People* (Nashville: Nelson Business, 2004), audio book, disk 1.

page 180   "Confrontational notes and e-mails are akin to manure bombs": Thom and Joani Schultz, *Friendship First* (Loveland, Colo.: Group, 2005), p. 71.

pages 180-81 Peter Scazzero identifies five unhealthy ways of dealing: From Peter Scazzero, *The Emotionally Healthy Church: A Strategy for Discipleship That Ac-*

tually Changes Lives (Grand Rapids: Zondervan, 2003), p. 103.

pages 182-83   Doug Fields gives new youth workers some of the best advice: The following statements are from Doug Fields, *Your First Two Years in Youth Ministry*
(El Cajon, Calif.: Youth Specialties, 2002), pp. 157, 158, 161.

page 185   The study revealed that "40% of the study parents": Statistics from this
paragraph are quoted in Barbara Kingsolver, *High Tide in Tucson* (New
York: HarperCollins, 1995), pp. 94-95.

page 187   As far back as 1996, 1,300 ministers: Frank Harrington, quoting the *At-
lanta Journal-Constitution* in a sermon at Peachtree Presbyterian Church,
October 20, 1996.

Chapter 13: Rabbit Trails and Brick Walls

page 188   "Spontaneity" is often mistaken for "fresh": Doug Fields, "Fresh-Smelling
Youth Ministry," *Group Magazine,* November-December 2006, p. 34.

page 195   three consistent components in winning organizations: Rosabeth Moss Kanter,
Confidence: How Winning Streaks and Losing Streaks Begin and End (New York:
Crown Business, 2004), p. 48.

Epilogue: Seizing the Unfair Advantage

page 204   "New life comes slowly, awkwardly, on wobbly wings": Sue Monk Kidd,
When the Heart Waits: Spiritual Direction for Life's Sacred Questions (San
Francisco: Harper & Row, 1990), p. 177.

page 204   "everything can look like a failure in the middle": Rosabeth Moss Kanter,
Confidence: How Winning Streaks and Losing Streaks Begin and End (New
York: Crown Business, 2004), p. 67.

Appendix A: Discussion Questions

page 209   Og Mandino argued that "the only certain means of success": Quoted in
Brian Tracy, *Eat That Frog! 21 Great Ways to Stop Procrastinating and Get
More Done in Less Time* (San Francisco: Berrett-Koehler Publishers, 2007),
p. 51.

Building Sustainable Ministries . . . One Church at a Time
www.ministryarchitects.com

Churches today face a tough reality: they desperately want to build thriving ministries, but the gap between aspiration and reality often feels insurmountable. Most simply resort to quick-fix solutions. These churches can easily become mired in a climate of criticism and complaint, as leaders and parents and pastors become increasingly obsessed with finding simple and immediate solutions.

But thriving, sustainable ministries are not built just because well-meaning leaders cobble together a disjointed collection of ideas from the most popular models, books and seminars. No, sustainable ministries take place when the church takes the time to "build the dance floor."

At Ministry Architects, we believe there is a better way—a better way than one-size-fits-all training events and quick-fix searches for super-star staffers. It all starts with building intentionally.

We have no interest in telling churches what they want to build. We start by listening and together develop a blueprint for moving from where they are to where they want to be. Then we walk alongside them to ensure that the renovation takes place in a sustainable way.

Ministry Architects partners with churches and their various ministries, working alongside key stakeholders to customize strategic plans for building successful and sustainable ministries.

For information about Ministry Architects or to schedule an assessment or other consulting services, visit ministryarchitects.com or contact us at info@ministryarchitects.com or 877-462-5718.